STRANGE BUT TRUE
San Francisco

STRANGE BUT TRUE
San Francisco
TALES OF THE CITY BY THE BAY

Lisa Montanarelli and Ann Harrison

INSIDERS' GUIDE®

GUILFORD, CONNECTICUT
AN IMPRINT OF THE GLOBE PEQUOT PRESS

Produced in 2005 by
PRC Publishing
The Chrysalis Building
Bramley Road, London W10 6SP, UK

An imprint of **Chrysalis** Books Group plc

Cover design: Sean Walsh
Text design: Sean Walsh
Photo credits: front cover © Chrysalis Image Library/Simon Clay

Library of Congress Cataloging-in-Publication Data available on request.

ISBN 0-7627-3681-X

Printed in Malaysia
First Edition/First Printing

STRANGE BUT TRUE
San Francisco

Introduction

San Francisco has always been a strange city. Its citizens live on the edge both geographically and culturally. From its beginnings as a tiny frontier town on the northernmost fringe of the Spanish empire, it has lured adventurers, speculators, and oddballs. When restless wanderers heard, "Go West, young man," thousands did just that. They collided at the far side of the continent and formed a wild city that still draws the unconventional.

Though Spain claimed California in 1542, Europeans didn't find the San Francisco Bay until 1769. Early explorers, like Sir Francis Drake, kept getting lost in the fog. When the Spanish finally found the bay and marveled at its natural harbor and mild climate, they forced the native Ohlone people to build a fort and a Mission church. Unlike the pious pilgrims who sailed to New England fleeing religious persecution, people came to California largely to escape religion: "They came not for conscience, but for coin," as one long-forgotten preacher said in 1894. Early Mexican residents named the place Yerba Buena or "good grass."

According to traditional U.S. history, James Marshall discovered gold near San Francisco in January 1848—the same month the U.S. officially wrested California from Mexico. As it turns out, Washington, D.C. knew about California's gold by May 4, 1846. Seven days later the U.S. invaded Mexico, supposedly due to a border dispute. President Polk waited until the time was right to show Congress the sparkling gold nugget that launched the California gold rush, on December 5, 1848.

The gold rush sparked a stampede of wanderers, misfits, ex-convicts, escaped former slaves, and other people wanting to shed their past and start over. The first "miner forty-niners" came from Peru and Chile. In 1849, the city, now renamed San Francisco, had its population rocket from 900 to 35,000. Rotting hulks of hundreds of abandoned ships filled the harbor as both passengers and crews hightailed it to the mines. People thought speculator James Lick was crazy when he bought the sand dunes and a cowpath behind the settlers' tents. But when the gold rush hit, Lick owned main street and became a land baron. Merchants, like blue jean impresario Levi Strauss, also made a fortune outfitting the miners.

Tens of thousands of Chinese immigrants joined the pursuit of riches. Fortune-seekers sifted millions of dollars worth of gold from the hills, and pinches of gold dust became the local currency. But fate is fickle on the golden shore. John Augustus Sutter, who owned gold-rich land, lost everything as desperate prospectors trampled his crops, ate his cattle, and ripped apart his buildings. He died a pauper.

With the boomtown economy came equally prosperous black markets, catering to the needs of a largely bachelor population. San Francisco became a favored port of rum runners and drug smugglers. Men outnumbered women a hundred to one, and most of the women were very high-spirited. In 1849, San Francisco had only 300 female citizens, 200 of whom were Mexican, Peruvian, and Chilean prostitutes. The next year another 2,000 ladies of easy virtue sailed into town, giving rise to the Barbary Coast, the nation's largest and most notorious red-light district. The city became a capital of naughty entertainment, pandering to every imaginable desire. Famous brothel keepers like Madame Marcelle amassed fortunes, built fine homes, and became the toast of society. One customer arrived early each morning at Madame Marcelle's Parisian Mansion, changed into women's clothes, swept and dusted the entire building, left a silver dollar on the parlor table, and departed. Madame Marcelle never revealed his name.

The city also witnessed periodic law and order crusades. Early San Francisco was awash with robberies, murders, and other crimes. Hoards of cutthroats and felons from the British penal colonies in Australia overwhelmed local authorities. Citizens took the law into their own hands. In the 1850s, they formed two Vigilance Committees in an effort to restore order. Swarms of armed vigilantes captured criminals, demanded the handover of inmates at the city jail, and strung up notorious outlaws such as English Jim. But the anti-vice campaigns did little to curb the thriving underworld. They merely helped advertise San Francisco as a "wide-open town."

The influx of itinerant dreamers and outlaws made San Francisco a magnet for nonconformists. The city celebrated eccentrics like Joshua Norton, one of many speculators who made a fortune in the boom or bust economy only to lose it overnight. Instead of shooting himself, as many ruined fortune seekers did, Norton proclaimed himself "Emperor of the United States and Protector of Mexico." For 30 years, most of San Francisco recognized his faux sovereignty. The local papers published his edicts. The State Senate reserved him a seat and often gave him the floor. When banks refused to lend Norton money, he minted his own currency, stamped with the image of his face. Most merchants accepted it. When the emperor died in 1890, 30,000 loyal subjects followed his funeral procession. San Franciscans still make yearly pilgrimages to his grave.

Along with its appreciation for the absurd, the city has a long history of graft and political corruption. Machine politics peaked in the early 1900s when political boss Abe Ruef wormed his way into the labor party and won behind-the-scenes control of the city. Crusading newspaper editor Fremont Older mounted an investigation of Ruef and his puppet, Mayor Eugene Schmitz. But just as things looked dicey for the politicos, a massive earthquake shook San Francisco. The 1906 quake threw people out of bed, toppled buildings, and ruptured the water mains needed by fire crews. Broken chimneys and burst gas lines sparked fires that merged into one giant blaze, reaching 2,700 degrees Fahrenheit. In three days, the flames consumed 2,593 acres—two-thirds of the city—and left 250,000 people homeless and more than 700 dead or missing. The fire marched across the city for days and was only stopped when the army seized buildings along Van Ness Avenue and blew them up to create a firebreak. Much of the evidence against Mayor Schmitz conveniently burned up in the fire. He and Ruef became heroes after the earthquake, but were later indicted for graft.

Since the 1906 quake, San Francisco has learned to take disaster in stride. The Barbary Coast bounced back almost overnight. While an act of the California Supreme Court officially closed the brothels in 1917, the party raged on. Prohibition did little to suppress the free flow of liquor, and San Francisco was known as the "wettest of the west." At the 1920 Democratic National Convention, municipal leaders scored a carload of the finest bourbon whiskey, which dazzled delegates accustomed to "paint remover and sheep dip." Elegant ladies greeted delegates at their hotels with free quart bottles, compliments of Mayor "Sunny Jim" Rolph.

San Francisco's shady history and foggy streets made it an ideal setting for detective stories. Many of Dashiell Hammett's gritty thrillers—including *The Maltese Falcon* (1930)—take place in the City by the Bay. A plaque near the Stockton Street tunnel marks the exact spot where Brigid O'Shaughnessy gunned down Miles Archer in one of *The Maltese Falcon*'s best scenes. Sam Spade —played by Humphrey Bogart in the film version—is Hammett's best-known sleuth. But true Hammett fans prefer the unnamed operative or "op" who worked for the Continental Detective Agency, a fictitious bureau based on the Pinkerton Detective Agency, in San Francisco where the author worked as a detective in real life. *The Big Knockover* (1927) takes place in the city's financial district, where bad guys target a string of banks on Montgomery Street. Hammett fans can take walking tours around San Francisco to visit the scenes of crimes portrayed in his books.

Fictional detectives were often based on local tough guys, like police inspector Jack Manion, who inspired many pulp detective stories of the 1920s and 1930s. In the 1920s, Manion supposedly negotiated a truce between the Chinese Tongs, whose gang war left scores of victims dead in the back alleys of Chinatown.

Another colorful character, millionaire publisher William Randolph Hearst, became proprietor of the *San Francisco Examiner* in 1887 at age 23. His father, George Hearst, had acquired the newspaper as payment for a gambling debt. Inspired by Joseph Pulitzer, Hearst turned the paper into a beacon of charging investigative journalism and lurid tabloid reporting. He hired some of the best writers around, including Mark Twain, Ambrose Bierce, Stephen Crane, and Jack London, who was born in nearby Oakland.

In 1931, Hearst tried to do his part for San Francisco's mushrooming tourist industry by purchasing the stones of a thirteenth-century Spanish monastery. Hearst meant to rebuild the monastery near the city, but he lost too much money in the financial collapse and had to abandon the plan. In 1937, the art deco Golden Gate Bridge joined San Francisco to nearby Marin County—unfortunately this spectacular structure soon became the world's most popular suicide site. The World's Fair brought still more tourists to town in 1939. Not satisfied with small gestures, the city created a new landmass, dredging the bay and building 400-acre Treasure Island. In the mid 1930s, another famous island in the bay, Alcatraz—also known as "the Rock"—hosted such maximum-security guests as Machine Gun Kelly and Al Capone. No one is known to have escaped Alcatraz alive, although some tried.

The San Francisco tourist trade catered to a wide variety of tastes. Following the 1933 repeal of Prohibition, lesbian and gay bars flourished in North Beach, once the site of the infamous Barbary Coast. Police tolerated these establishments because they drew tourist dollars.

In World War II, the San Francisco harbor served as the port of embarkation for the war in the Pacific. As during the gold rush, thousands of single men flooded the city's saloons and brothels. Women got a taste of emancipation and took over men's jobs in the nearby Oakland shipyards, giving birth to the legend of Rosie the Riveter. World War II also left the city with an unsolved mystery and one of the first theories of UFO abduction. On August 1942, Navy Airship Squadron blimp L-8 took off from Treasure Island at 6:03 A.M. When the blimp crashed south of San Francisco five hours later, the door was latched open, and both crewmembers had vanished. Some people say that aliens kidnapped them.

Meanwhile, back in North Beach, another form of alien culture took root in the bars and coffeehouses. There, at the edge of the world's edgiest city, beatniks penned controversial poetry. The godmother of the beats, San Francisco poet Helen Adams, supposedly made mist rise as she chanted her poems at local readings. Beat culture shared the stage with the emerging folk music scene. In October of 1955, beat poet Allen Ginsberg read his famous poem *Howl*, kicking off what beat author Jack Kerouac dubbed the San Francisco Renaissance. Local police later arrested his publisher on obscenity charges.

While the beats sampled mind-expanding drugs, the CIA instigated their own experiments in San Francisco. In 1953, the agency launched the MK-ULTRA program to study the effects of LSD and its potential use as a mind-control weapon. Two years later, CIA agent George Hunter White opened Operation Midnight Climax in San Francisco. White hired prostitutes to pick up men from local bars, slip them LSD, and bring them back to a federally funded brothel on Telegraph Hill. Seated behind a two-way mirror, White sipped martinis and watched the men cope with the effects of the LSD.

Some San Francisco Bay Area hospitals also recruited willing subjects, for government-sponsored LSD studies. Both Ginsberg and author Ken Kesey volunteered for these research projects, ingesting LSD then using the drug for their own explorations. Kesey called it the "revolt of the guinea pigs." By the mid '60s, mind-morphing psychedelics had sparked Dionysian revelry and cultural revolution. Kesey and his Merry Pranksters staged their own "acid tests." The hippie counterculture flowered in Haight-Ashbury, San Francisco's psychedelic district. Across the bay in Berkeley, the Free Speech Movement took off in October 1964 at the University of California. Injecting politics into psychedelia, San Francisco hippie Michael Bowen inspired the March on the Pentagon. In October 1967, 75,000 protesters tried to halt the Vietnam War by encircling the Pentagon and levitating the building until it vibrated and turned orange. "Out! Demons out!" the demonstrators shouted.

San Francisco's cultural upheaval of the sixties sparked numerous other political causes: Black Power, Native American Pride, the New Left, environmentalism, feminism, gay rights, anti-nuclear protests, Latin American solidarity, AIDS activism, and numerous other movements all trace their lineage to this magical time and place.

The city still draws iconoclasts and contemporary pranksters, such as the culture jammers of the Billboard Liberation Front. Spontaneous lunacies still arise—one day in 1991, a four-foot granite traffic barrier mysteriously appeared in Golden Gate Park. Within a few weeks, people began to leave flowers and burn incense around the traffic plug. Some hailed it as "Shiva Linga"—the stone phallus of the Hindu god Shiva—and claimed it possessed miraculous healing powers. Others thought San Franciscans had once again gone nuts. In 2004, Haight-Ashbury locals subverted city efforts to establish a traffic circle at the intersection of Scott and Waller Streets by installing a gold-painted toilet—a shrine to bad traffic planning—in the middle of the roundabout.

The recent burst of the dot-com bubble shows that the city can still ride out its capricious boom or bust economies. Private property values have skyrocketed. Downtown condominiums now sell for more than a million dollars. Gay rights has branched into multiple gay movements, and for one month in 2004, San Francisco granted nearly 4,000 same-sex couples the right to marry, sparking a nationwide debate that took a front seat in the 2004 presidential election. Earthquakes—both seismic and social—have come and gone. Residents form local committees to prepare for the Big One that seismologists predict. In the meantime, tourism still fuels the city's economy, prostitutes agitate for decriminalization and respect, and the city celebrates its eccentrics. Police recently arrested a man at Fisherman's Wharf for twisting himself into nude yoga postures. The city declined to prosecute because, alas, there is no law against nude yoga in San Francisco.

PART I:
Strange But True

It is an odd thing, but every one who disappears is said to be seen at San Francisco. It must be a delightful city and possess all the attractions of the next world.

— Oscar Wilde

San Francisco is a mad city, inhabited for the most part by perfectly insane people whose women are of a remarkable beauty.

— Rudyard Kipling

Fact is often stranger than fiction in the twisted streets of San Francisco. From its origins as a boomtown of crazed gold miners, the city has weathered the weird winds of fortune. In 1849, 35,000 rowdy miners transformed a sleepy Mexican settlement into a playground for newly rich bachelors. Exponential population growth left so few places to sleep that early landlords made large fortunes renting bunks, tabletops, and rocking chairs at outrageous prices. As gold rush millionaires replaced their teeth with solid gold dentures, one dentist got so rich that he erected statues to himself all over the city. Unusual? Not in this town.

As the city grew, the chaos did too. The mud plague of 1850 turned the streets into sinkholes that swallowed wagons, animals, and unfortunate pedestrians whose bodies were lost for weeks. Citizens converted the abandoned ships clogging the harbor into bars, prisons, and insane asylums. Rotting hulks formed the city's first landfill, which now lies beneath the downtown. Notoriously corrupt San Francisco politicians won elections with free food, equestrian expertise, and bribery. The first women in San Francisco were mostly harlots, and bawdy entertainment drove the city's economy until 1900. In 1890 alone, the city issued liquor licenses to 3,117 bars—one for every 96 citizens. High liquor consumption did not prevent the astonishingly robust members of the Dolphin Club from swimming all night in the 50-degree waters of the bay—a strange practice they have continued from 1877 to this day.

The fire following the 1906 earthquake inspired more strange feats. As the city burned down around her, madam Jessie Hayman remained open for business, moving her girls from house to house, steps ahead of the advancing flames. Hundreds—perhaps thousands—perished in the earthquake and fire, but several years later, the Board of Supervisors evicted the dead, exiling all cemeteries to Colma, south of San Francisco.

Other strange tales include that of the esteemed anthropologist who rescued a starving native man only to make him into a museum display and pickle his brain when he died. In 1941, the KGB set up a covert office in San Francisco to hunt down defectors: They code-named the place Babylon, of course. Entertainer Carol Doda launched the topless dancing craze in San Francisco and promptly ensured her breasts for $1.5 million. On a sadder note, so many people jumped off the Golden Gate Bridge that local newspapers kept a weekly count.

The KGB code-named the place Babylon, of course.

Built on landfill and seismic faultlines, San Francisco remains stable in its instability, enduring constant flux. Residents brave plagues of giant flying cockroaches in Golden Gate Park, man-eating sharks offshore, and a sinister ring of flesh-eating plant smugglers. Strangely resilient, San Franciscans seek ever new horizons of lunacy. In the last decade alone there have been many strange events—the city has survived the dot-com boom; new entrepreneurs have cloned pets; and researchers have monitored local goat herds for radioactivity. They have not tried to clone the goats yet.

Toilet-Seat Guitars

Some people brainstorm best while sitting on the john. In 1968, Charlie Deal realized "he might be sitting on a great musical idea." In the sleepy town of Mill Valley, just north of San Francisco, Deal began to build guitars out of toilet seats. He has made 115 working models since 1968.

However, when he tried to patent his invention, the U.S. patent office claimed it was nothing more than a modified part of the commode. Deal had to play the guitar in order to prove it actually worked. He now holds two patents, and one of his toilet-seat guitars appears on the album cover of *Sports* by Huey Lewis and the News.

Isadora Duncan's Dramatic Life and Death

Isadora Duncan, born in San Francisco on May 27, 1878, lived by the motto *sans limites* [without limits]. She grew up in a poor, artistic family on the corner of Taylor and Geary Streets and began teaching dance at 14. Rejecting the strictures of classical ballet, Duncan danced barefoot, with free-flowing theatrical movements. In Europe, she first gained recognition for what later became known as the art of modern dance, but she was considered a bit too quirky for early 20th-century America. According to one critic, the diaphanous silk tunics that she wore on stage could have gotten her arrested for indecent exposure.

Duncan championed women's rights, free love, and the Bolshevik Revolution, while she opposed matrimony, which she called a "highly overrated performance." She shocked U.S. audiences by touring while obviously pregnant but unmarried. Duncan knew many famous artists and writers of her day and had many lovers. One night, F. Scott Fitzgerald flirted with Duncan, making his wife Zelda so jealous that she threw herself down a flight of stairs.

> The freakish accident that took Duncan's life on the Riviera was so dramatic... that many believed she had staged it herself.

Duncan had two children, Deirdre and Patrick. In 1913, while performing in Paris, she had numerous presentiments of an approaching death, which she thought was her own. Once she went into a trance on stage. "She seems to be dancing in the face of death. Truly she has death before her," remarked one of her friends. Days later, her children and their governess were driving near the Seine when the car stalled, facing the river. When the chauffeur got out to crank the engine, the car lurched forward, jumped the curb, and plunged into the water—with the children and their nurse screaming inside. Though Duncan never truly recovered, she threw herself wholeheartedly into the alternative dance schools for underprivileged children that she had founded years earlier. She later adopted six female students who toured with her as "The Isadorables."

The freakish accident that took Duncan's life on the Riviera in 1927 was so dramatic and in character that many believed she had staged it herself. One clear September evening, she went for a drive dressed in her trademark outfit—a long red silk scarf wrapped repeatedly around her neck and body. Climbing into the passenger seat of a Bugatti sports car, she tossed the scarf once more around her neck, and cried, *Adieu, mes amis, je vais à la gloire!* [Good-bye, my friends, I go to glory!]

As she sat down, the fringes of her scarf fell outside the car and caught in the spokes of the rear wheel. Duncan's friend Mary barely had time to shout, "Isadora, your shawl!" before the Bugatti sped off. Seconds later, the wheel's force dragged Duncan out of the car and hurled her onto the street. She died instantly, a true victim of fashion.

400 Robots Test Their Mettle in Olympic-Style Games

In March 2004, robot athletes from 11 nations, including Australia, Canada, Germany, and Japan, came to San Francisco for the first international Robolympics. They competed in events such as soccer, line slalom, boxing, sumo wrestling, maze-solving, and even firefighting. While Japanese robots took the gold, silver, and bronze in heavyweight sumo wrestling (both autonomous and remote control), the American machines specialized in demolishing the living hell out of each other in one-on-one robot combat. They competed in weight classes from one to 340 pounds. Some biped androids practiced kung-fu, ballet, jump rope, and tumbling. But many contestants were not humanoid. For instance, super-heavyweight Blue Max was a 340-pound rectangle with four wheels and a wedge for smashing other robots. Canadian David Hrynkiw designed some autonomous mini-sumo wrestlers who—unlike their hefty human counterparts —weighed barely more than a pound.

The toughest event was robot soccer, which had five robots per team. A camera suspended above the playing field sent signals to each team's computer. From this, the computer determined where the ball was, where the robots were, and where they needed to go. It then sent a wireless signal to the robots.

The Robotics Society of America (RSA) hosted the event. RSA president David Calkins said only 20 percent of the robot designers were professional engineers. The others, including a hundred kids, were simply enthusiasts and hobbyists. "This is where they come to show off their wares. It's testing your mettle," said Calkins.

The Grand Dame of Conspiracy Theories

If San Francisco is a city awash with conspiracy theories, it could be because gemologist Bruce Porter Roberts scrawled the infamous *Gemstone File* here. The manuscript was written at 895 Bush Street in a little Tenderloin District bar, The Drift Inn—now called Yong San Lounge. In 350 to 1,000 handwritten pages of mad rant, Roberts claims to unveil the secret, government-suppressed history of the United States' rise to global power following World War II. He manages to tie the CIA, the FBI, the JFK and Bobby Kennedy assassinations, Jackie O., Howard Hughes, Richard Nixon, Watergate, Chappaquiddik, Ted Kennedy, Mary Jo Kopechne, San Francisco Mayor Joe Alioto, and numerous other billionaires, spies, and scandalous events into one sprawling tabloid conspiracy, spearheaded by the international Mafia and Aristotle Onassis.

The story goes like this: Roberts invented the synthetic ruby now used in laser technology. In 1960, Hughes Aircraft supposedly stole his rubies for laser weapons research. As Roberts investigated the theft, he discovered that the crime was part of a vast network of geopolitical intrigue. Roberts, his gems, and even his corner bar, The Drift Inn, played a crucial role in this secret world history that the government sought to suppress by whatever means necessary.

Roberts spent 15 years—until his death in 1976—writing the *Gemstone File*. He first revealed the manuscript in 1969. According to *Gemstone*, Onassis and the international Mafia abducted defense industry mogul Howard Hughes and held him captive for 10 years. They concealed the kidnapping by replacing the real Hughes with a double. Onassis then used Hughes's empire to hijack the U.S. government without anyone knowing that Onassis had staged a coup and was now behind the wheel. He had John and Robert Kennedy shot when they rebelled against him. After JFK's death, Jackie married Onassis to protect her children from a similar fate. (This may sound like a familiar tale. In his book *Inside the Gemstone File* (1999), David Hatcher Childress suggests that the James Bond movie *Diamonds Are Forever* (1972) was based on *Gemstone* or a similar theory.)

The story gets even nuttier. Roberts says G. Gordon Liddy first plotted the Watergate burglary at The Drift Inn in San Francisco. The Arabs, Chinese, and Russians wired the bar and listened in as Roberts traded phony gems with CIA spooks for bits of information. Even the bartender worked as a spy for the *Washington Post*.

If this sounds like paranoid schizophrenia, it probably is. Some people swear by the *Gemstone File*, but many others think it's bunk. Very little of it corresponds with known geopolitical history. Plus, countless references to cannibalism cast doubt on its veracity. Nonetheless, the *Gemstone File* (or rather the 24-page *Skeleton Key*, penned in 1975) has been enshrined in the canon of conspiracy literature and now serves as a touchstone for the genre—spawning other grand narratives linking wildly disparate events in a unified theory of everything. The document has likewise conspired to make San Francisco the capital of conspiracy theory, for better or for worse.

Giant Roaches Invade Wedding

One of San Francisco's loveliest party settings once witnessed a grotesque wedding calamity. The Conservatory of Flowers, located in Golden Gate Park, is the oldest glass-and-wood Victorian greenhouse in the Western Hemisphere. Built in 1879, it houses more than 10,000 exotic plants from around the world. In 1995, the conservatory closed for eight years and underwent a $25 million restoration.

Shortly before the greenhouse closed, it hosted a fateful wedding. After tying the knot, the bride and groom adjourned to another room in the conservatory to cut the cake—and found it crawling with giant Australian cockroaches. The bride ran screaming from the building.

The staff at the conservatory couldn't figure out where the giant Australian cockroaches came from. Unlike the common German roaches that lurk in San Francisco kitchens, the giant Australians are not native to northern California—and they can fly.

Experts suspect they hitchhiked a ride to the conservatory on exotic plants. In any case, the flying fist-sized bugs seemed immune to the low-toxicity baits used against their smaller cousins, and the glasshouse managers feared that stronger insecticides would be toxic to both plants and visitors.

After much deliberation, they decided to import natural predators. The conservatory acquired 20 gecko lizards, blessed with voracious appetites, sticky feet, a distinctive call, and a fondness for licking their own eyeballs. The managers later added smaller lizards called anoles, which change colors like chameleons. Though the lizards were much smaller than their cockroach prey, they found the meaty yet tender cockroaches quite a delicacy.

"If they can fit it into their mouths, they'll try to eat it," said Julie Bergman, the owner of the Gecko Ranch in Davis, California. Bergman helped supply the conservatory with three varieties of geckos from among the 55 species she raises.

The natural balance of terror inside the glasshouse has apparently worked. Those who now visit the conservatory's Highland Tropics collection and the aquatic plants display—which includes giant lily pads that can support the weight of a small child—may encounter the geckos. They tend to blend in with the other fauna, including the 800 live butterflies fluttering inside the building. No word yet on whether the geckos have also developed a taste for butterflies.

Furry Products

John Sperling shares his mansion in San Francisco's Pacific Heights district with unusual pets. His two kittens, Tabouli and Baba Ganoush, are identical clones of their "donor mom," Tahini, a Bengal cat who donated skin cells for the project.

According to the *San Francisco Chronicle*, Sperling is backing the world's first pet-cloning business. The firm, Genetic Savings and Clone, created Tabouli and Baba Ganoush as sample copycats.

Sperling's kittens—the second and third cat clones in the world—were born to separate surrogate mothers. They apparently have none of the health problems common to cloned animals. Since their birth, they have toured the country, appearing in cat shows.

Genetic Savings and Clone is filling orders for other cloned cats. The company offers a money-back guarantee or a free clone if their furry products have any genetic defects. Several hundred clients have paid the firm $900 plus a $150 annual fee to "bank" tissue from their dog or cat for future cloning.

The inspiration for the company came from Sperling's desire to clone his beloved husky dog Missy, who died in 2002. The *Chronicle* does not record whether Sperling banked his husky dog's cells in order to produce future Missys.

Humphrey the Lost Whale

In October 1985, an 80,000-pound, 40-foot humpback whale was migrating from Alaska to Mexico when he took a wrong turn into the bay, passed into the Carquinez Strait, and dead-ended at Rio Vista, halfway between Sacramento and

San Francisco. For the next 25 days, the whale made a splash across the world's news channels, as scientists puzzled over how to lure the creature out of the Delta. They finally succeeded by playing underwater recordings of other humpbacks feeding. On November 4, Humphrey swam through the Golden Gate back into the Pacific Ocean.

Men Smuggle Flesh-Eating Plants

On April 15, 1995, three members of the Bay Area Carnivorous Plant Society pleaded guilty to smuggling more than 200 flesh-eating plants from Asia into the U.S. Fellow carnivorous plant lovers understood the smugglers' motives. "Carnivorous plants can really give you an obsession," said one. "It just grabs hold of you once you start growing these plants. I started out with a Venus flytrap 35 years ago . . . You get one and you want another one." Reporting for the *San Francisco Examiner*, Tanya Schevitz explains that many of the society's members "were first drawn to the flesh-eating plants by a childhood fascination with the Venus flytrap's spiked mouths." She describes one member's backyard: "Small tentacles sprout from the dozens of pots . . . (More) mature carnivorous plants . . . lurk in the greenhouse he built when his collection began overtaking the windowsills."

Sharks Taste-Test Humans

The Red Triangle—reaching from Tomales Bay to Monterey Bay to the Farallon Islands, 28 miles west of San Francisco—is one of the most popular surf sites in the whole of the U.S. The region also boasts the world's highest incidence of white shark attacks. From 1926 through 2000, there have been 51 shark attacks—five of them fatal.

Most are not deadly, because sharks tend to taste-test their prey before gobbling it whole. Sharks have bad eyesight and cannot tell the difference between a seal and a surfer in a wet suit. They often spit out humans, who are much bonier than seals and their other favorite foods. They frequently taste-test surfboards too.

On a sunny Sunday afternoon in August 2004, fisheries activist Randy Fry and his old friend Cliff Zimmerman were snorkeling in 15 feet of water off Fort Bragg, north of San Francisco. As they searched for abalone above a kelp bed about 150 feet offshore, Zimmerman heard a whooshing sound and felt the pressure of something very large moving between him and Fry. The water suddenly filled with blood, and Fry disappeared.

The next day, the Coast Guard found a headless body on the ocean floor and the body was identified as Fry's: It wore a wet suit with his name on it. A few weeks later, beachcombers found Fry's head washed up on the shore. Fry was the western regional director for the Recreational Fishing Alliance, a group that brings together recreational anglers, commercial fishermen, and lobbies for marine preservation. Zimmerman said he and Fry discussed sharks many times. "He said, 'I think a shark will get me sometime,'" Zimmerman told the Cyber Diver News Network. "It's common banter among abalone divers."

According to the California Department of Fish and Game, the California coast has seen 106 shark attacks on humans in the last 50 years. Ten of these attacks have been fatal. The last before Fry's disappearance occurred 350 miles south on Avila Beach in August 2003. In that incident, university professor Deborah Franzman bled to death when a great white shark attacked her during her morning swim.

Datura: The First California Psychedelic

Hallucinogens were popular in the San Francisco area long before the 1960s. *Datura stramonium*, a white-flowered plant the Aztecs called *toloatzin* or *toloache*, grows wild in the American west. The indigenous Californians used it as a psychedelic narcotic in religious rituals and healing practices. Though the *toloache* religion is older and more common in southern California, the natives of the San Francisco Bay used *datura* as well.

According to anthropologists Lowell Bean and Sylvia Vane, the plant is so poisonous that the Indians' ability to dose people without killing them marks "a significant technological achievement." Stephen Schwartz writes, "While the Indian use of *datura* does not explain the mass drug-taking that emerged in California in the late 20th century, it provides a remarkable antecedent of the practice, and there are historical links, slender but real, between the two phenomena."

San Francisco's Buffalo Herd

In the 1890s, Golden Gate Park featured an open-range zoo populated with elk, bears, goats, and other beasts. All that remains is a buffalo paddock containing a small herd of bison. At the time of this writing, the herd included 12 females and two male yearlings, all descended from a cow named Madame Sarah Bernhardt and a bull named Ben Harrison.

Seven of the bison came down with bovine tuberculosis in 1980 and were transferred to an enclosure near the San Francisco county jail in San Bruno.

A group of citizens called the Watchbison Committee looks after the bison. Members form work parties to weed the bison paddock. They once gathered 480 signatures on a petition entreating the San Francisco Zoo not to

> *They once gathered 480 signatures on a petition entreating officials not to send an undersized female bison, "Runt," to the Detroit Zoo.*

send an undersized female bison, known as the Runt, to the Detroit Zoo. The petition succeeded, and Runt happily remained with the herd.

San Francisco is a golden handcuff with the key thrown away.

– John Steinbeck

Radioactive Goats?

The lab at the University of California at Berkeley measures background levels of radiation by testing a nearby herd of 50 to 300 goats. Conducting nuclear research, the lab tracks airborne radionuclides such as tritium, a hydrogen isotope that emits low-level beta radiation. So far the lab has not detected high tritium levels in the goats' dung or milk, but, just in case, the herd's owner does not sell the goats' milk for human consumption. The lab also deploys the goats around the area to eat shrubs that might otherwise fuel a brush fire. Researchers draw elaborate maps of their grazing patterns. It's comforting to think that in the most technologically-advanced economy, there is still a place for a goat herder.

The Church of All Worlds

From 1980 to 1984 the Church of All Worlds, a Bay Area neo-pagan group, raised and exhibited "living unicorns." The founder Oberon Zell and his partner

Morning Glory Zell surgically produced the one-horned creatures by operating on baby goats. Oberon publishes *Green Egg: A Journal of the Awakening Earth*, a publication catering to the pagan community. In 1977, the Zells formed a church subsidiary, the Ecosophical Research Association, to investigate the roots of legends and myths. In addition to rearing unicorns, the group has searched for mermaids off the coast of New Guinea.

Escape From Alcatraz

On June 11, 1962, Clarence and John Anglin and Frank Lee Morris escaped from Alcatraz. The inmates spent months digging out the ventilator grills at the rear of their cells. Using more than 50 raincoats collected from other prisoners, they patched together homemade rafts and life preservers. The week before their escape, the Anglin brothers molded dummy heads with homemade clay made of toilet paper and soap. They left the heads in their bunks to fool the guards, while they slipped through the ventilators to freedom.

The three prisoners planned to reach the mainland by rafting across the San Francisco Bay, which surrounds Alcatraz. No one ever saw or heard from them again. Temperatures in the bay range from 50- to 54-degrees Fahrenheit. In such cold water, the convicts would have died of hypothermia in two to three hours. Their bodies were never recovered, but personal items and a life preserver with teeth marks around the valve were found floating in the bay the next day.

The only other prisoners to attempt the escape from Alcatraz were Theodore Cole and Ralph Rose in 1937. They may have drowned in the Bay as well, although their bodies were never recovered.

Swimmers in the Icy Water

Members of the Dolphin Club (www.dolphinclub.org) have been swimming in the bone-chilling, polluted waters of the San Francisco Bay since 1877. Many of the 900 members swim year-round in a bay lagoon known as Aquatic Park—with water temperatures ranging from 50 degrees Fahrenheit in January to 61 degrees in September.

The club also holds an annual Escape from Alcatraz Triathalon, including a one-and-a-half-mile swim (without wet suit) from Alcatraz Island to Aquatic Park, followed by a 14-mile bike ride across the Golden Gate Bridge to Mill Valley and a 13-mile run over Mount Tamalpais to Stinson Beach and back over the mountain.

If swimming in the bay isn't enough of a feat in itself, the Web site lists the other accomplishments of some of the club members. In 1967, Lieutenant Colonel Stewart Evans became the first and only person ever to swim 19.57 miles from the Farallon Islands to Point Bolinas. Evans began swimming in the 56-degree water at 10:17 P.M. on August 27 and finished at noon the next day.

In 1974, fitness guru Jack LaLanne towed a rowboat from Alcatraz to the Dolphin Club in less than 90 minutes while wearing shackles and manacles like an escaped convict.

Famed Author Hoards Junk

In May 1996, the Saroyan Foundation gave Stanford University the literary legacy and effects of the late Oscar- and Pulitzer Prize-winning author William Saroyan. The collection includes 1,500 cardboard boxes containing Saroyan's unpublished work, as well as thousands of hoarded items such as newspapers, subway tickets, rocks, matchbook covers, labels peeled off cans, and a plastic bag of 10,000 rubber bands. The decision "fulfills Saroyan's wish that his collection be kept in one spot."

The Toe Stalker

In April 1991, San Francisco State University reported three incidents of a man who allegedly entered the dormitories and attempted to lick women's legs and toes. In San Francisco, law-abiding foot fetishists have formed social groups and throw parties devoted to foot worship.

Poet Misplaces 38 Years

Famed poet William Carlos Williams was 71 and apparently losing his memory when he wrote the introduction to the 1956 Pocket Poets edition of beat poet Allen Ginsberg's *Howl and Other Poems*. According to Williams, Ginsberg—who first read *Howl* in San Francsico in 1955—was "disturbed by the life which he had encountered about him during those first years after the First World War . . . Now he turns up 15 or 20 years later with an arresting poem." The editors apparently didn't notice that 38 years had past since World War I. Ginsberg was born in 1926, eight years after World War I ended. Twenty years before the Pocket Poets edition of *Howl*, he would have been only 10 years old.

Bras Across the Grand Canyon

In the mid-1990s, Point Richmond artist Ronnie Nicolino tried to collect enough bras to complete his project *Bras Across the Grand Canyon*, "a politically designed project to convey how America is body and breast obsessed." Sadly, Nicolino was only able to gather 20,000 bras—far too few to string across the Grand Canyon —and the park service said no anyway.

Nicolino then came up with another idea: With 40,000 bras, he would construct the *National Bra Tapestry*, a 40- by 100-foot replica of the Statue of

Liberty, which would tour the nation. Nicolino would finally offer the *Tapestry* to President Clinton as a plea from women across the nation for more breast cancer research. Nicolino never completed this project either, but with the help of 200 volunteers, he brought together 21,000 size 34C bras to make a two-mile-long sand sculpture on Stinson Beach—just across the Golden Gate Bridge from San Francisco.

The BraBall Dispute

After the beach project, Nicolino was ready to give up his 20,000 bras, which were probably costing him a lot of money in storage. He posted an ad offering to donate his collection of female undergarments to another artist.

Emily Duffy, an artist from El Cerrito, contacted him. Duffy told Nicolino about her plan to create "a giant BraBall, something on the order of a rubber-band ball made of foundation garments." After talking and meeting several times, Duffy sent Nicolino sketches for a project that the two of them would supposedly work on together. She was shocked when Nicolino claimed the idea as his own and "issued a press release saying that he [was] beginning work immediately," crediting Duffy "for helping develop the BraBall idea." Duffy insisted she had copyrighted her sketches and went on to exhibit her own BraBall, while Nicolino's version never materialized.

Evicting the Dead

On March 26, 1900, San Francisco outlawed future burials within city limits. In 1912, the Board of Supervisors went one step further and announced their intent to evict all cemeteries in the city. In 1914, they sent eviction notices to the dead. Citizens fought the eviction for 23 years—that is, San Francisco's living inhabitants contested the order.

In 1937, the city won the right to evict the graveyards, and the dead had to go. Now, only the Mission Dolores Cemetery and the San Francisco National Cemetery at the Presidio remain within city limits. The rest of the internments were moved south of San Francisco to Colma, the nation's only incorporated city where the dead outnumber the living. In 1924, the Associated Cemeteries incorporated so the dead would never have to move again. Colma now houses 1,200 living residents and more than one million dead. A local bumper sticker gloats, "It's great to be alive in Colma."

Some headstones from San Francisco cemeteries never made it to Colma. Hundreds were dumped and buried at the city's Ocean Beach, 50 yards from the southern edge of the beach. In the 1970s, the beach highway was eroding and construction crews had to repair the road with sand from Ocean Beach. During the digging, they found the buried tombstones and moved them 2,000 feet farther down the beach. In San Francisco, you never know what's under your feet.

Wandering Stones

In 1931, the newspaper mogul and compulsive art collector William Randolph Hearst acquired an unusual piece for his art collection: the ruins of the 13th-century Trappist monastery of Santa María de Óvila in Spain. Though the ruins cost a mere $50,000, Hearst shelled out another $750,000 to pay a hundred stonemasons, carpenters, and unskilled laborers to dismantle and move the monastery to San Francisco. The job took one year.

The 9,000-plus stones spent the next 10 years at Haslett's San Francisco waterfront warehouse for a rent of $1,000 per month. Hearst planned to reconstruct the monastery near McCloud, California, but his overspending brought him near bankruptcy. In July 1941, he struck a deal with the City of San Francisco and traded the stones for payment of his outstanding storage fees.

The city stored the stones in a eucalyptus grove behind the Japanese Tea Garden with the intent of rebuilding the monastery in Golden Gate Park. The stones remained in the grove for 53 years. Factions quarreled over where to rebuild the monastery, and numerous mishaps delayed reconstruction. In 1959, vandals set fire to the eucalyptus and the heat and water pressure from the fire hoses cracked 80 percent of the stones, making them unfit for building. In 1969, the de Young Museum abandoned its plans to rebuild the monastery and allowed its pieces to be used for other purposes. Truckloads went to a children's playground in Oakland, and workers used them to build walls, pathways, and birdbaths in Golden Gate Park.

In 1991, the remaining stones of the Trappist monastery finally found a new vocation. Modern-day druids used them to build a Stonehenge-like rock garden around a four-foot granite traffic barrier that had mysteriously appeared behind the Japanese Tea Garden. Soon worshipers from around the world made pilgrimages to the traffic plug to pray and offer flowers and incense to "Shiva Linga," which some claimed possessed healing powers.

In November 1993, park officials decreed that it was illegal to build a religious shrine in a public park.

In November 1993, park officials decreed that it was illegal to build a religious shrine in a public park. After much ado, Harry Parker, director of the Fine Arts Museums of San Francisco, gave the 900 surviving stones from the monastery to the Trappist Abbey of New Clairvaux in Vina, California. The abbey intends to reconstruct the Chapter House. This time it looks like it might actually happen.

Woman Wrecks Buddhist Art

In the spring of 1991, a group of Tibetan monks made a sand painting representing the Buddist image of the "Wheel of Life" at the Asian Art Museum in Golden Gate Park. As the monks were arranging millions of colored grains of sand, a woman claiming CIA ties jumped the rope barrier and destroyed the painting—denouncing "Buddhist Death Cults" in front of 200 onlookers. The monks scattered the ruined sand in the ocean and calmly started over.

The Yellow Tide

The women of The Yellow Tide, based in San Francisco, protest against the excessive greed and environmental recklessness of the SUV-driving, dot-com generation that settled in the city in the late 1990s. The Yellow Tide women walk the streets in overcoats and stiletto heels. When they spot a shiny new sports utility vehicle, they open their overcoats, display their lingerie, and do unspeakable things to the spotless paint job.

Gin-Soaked City

In 1890, San Francisco granted liquor licenses to 3,117 businesses. This meant that for every 96 citizens of San Francisco, there was one new bar—and that wasn't counting the 2,000 or more illegal speakeasies that existed. Customers drank an estimated $9,000,000 worth of alcohol at the licensed bars that year alone.

Doda Launches Topless Craze

In 1964, Harvard University named Carol Doda "Businessperson of the Year" after she made history that June by gyrating on top of the white grand piano at San Francisco's Condor Club in nothing but a bikini bottom. The topless bar was born.

Condor manager Davey Rosenberg got the idea when he spotted a photo of a model in a topless swimsuit designed by Rudi Gernreich. His boss, Gino Del Prete, bought the swimsuit, and Doda did the dancing. Within 48 hours, waitresses at neighboring North Beach bars were baring their breasts—stopping traffic on Columbus and Broadway. Doda became famous for writhing on the Condor's white baby grand as it descended from the ceiling. Later that year she took silicone injections, enlarging her breasts from size 34 to 44, then insuring her breasts for $1.5 million with Lloyds of London. In 1983, the Condor Club again made news when, late one night, show dancer Theresa Hill and bouncer Jimmy Ferrozzo made out on top of the baby grand. The hydraulic mechanism jammed, and the piano rose, crushing Ferrozzo to death. Hill remained pinned underneath her dead boyfriend until the janitor found them.

San Francisco is 49 square miles surrounded by reality.

— Paul Kantner of the rock band Jefferson Airplane

Topless Dancer Chains Self to Bridge

In 1965, topless dancer Yvonne D'Angers chained herself to the Golden Gate Bridge to protest her upcoming deportation to Persia. Diane Arbus's 1968 photograph "Topless Dancer in Her Dressing Room" shows D'Angers—her breasts framed in sequins and feathers with a reproduction of Leonardo da Vinci's *Last Supper* in the background.

Splosh

Imagine rolling in a kiddie pool full of chocolate syrup in a room with 200 other people dousing themselves and each other in oatmeal, pudding, and strawberry jam. Bathing in food—also known as Splosh—was all the rage a few years ago in San Francisco. One of the authors of this book attended a Splosh party at a club called Spandango. She carried an umbrella, but even that didn't protect her from being pelted with food and smelling like confectioner's sugar for days afterward. The next time you find yourself wishing for something new in the fashion world, be careful what you wish for. They may start wearing food.

California: The Garden of Eden

Before European explorers had even discovered the West Coast of the New World, they imagined a racy and sumptuous garden of earthly delights called "California." The 16th-century Spanish conquistadors believed that the Garden of Eden was an actual place on the globe. One goal of their voyages was to find this "Earthly Paradise." The early explorers savored Garcí Rodríguez de Montalvo's *Exploits of the Very Zealous Knight Esplandián, Son of the Great King Amadis of Gaul.*

The book, written in 1500, describes a fictional island called California: "[At] the right hand of the Indes there was an island called California, very near the Earthly Paradise, which was peopled by black women without any man among them, so that their style of life was almost like that of the Amazons."

The women of Montalvo's California were rather fierce. They rode flying griffins and made their weapons out of gold—the only metal on the island. Their queen, Califía, led them into battle against Constantinople, where they captured men to use for breeding, slave labor, and griffin food.

Europeans believed California was an island until 1687, when Father Eusebio Francisco Kino, a German Jesuit, sailed down the Colorado River twice and convinced himself and others that California was attached to northern Mexico.

While the maps changed long ago, many people still view California as an island of sorts because its culture and geography remain so different from the rest of the U.S.

Early Explorers Lost in Fog

Lost in the fog that often covers San Francisco, European explorers sailed right past the San Francisco Bay and never saw it. Juan Rodriguez Cabrillo was the first to miss the bay in 1542. His pilot Bartolome Ferrelo sailed past it two more times, though he spotted the Farallon Islands.

In June 1579, Francis Drake also missed the San Francisco Bay, landing instead near Point Reyes, 25 miles north of San Francisco, in what is now called Drakes Bay.

In 1595, Sebastián Cermeño shipwrecked, probably in the same bay where Drake landed, and named it La Bahía de San Francisco. Two centuries later, explorers traveling over land finally stumbled upon the San Francisco Bay and assumed it was the harbor Cermeño had found. No one realized their mistake until 1775, when Juan Manuel de Ayala mapped the area.

Drake Gives Northern California to Queen Elizabeth

In 1579, Francis Drake landed on the northern California coast and claimed it for the British throne. He thought that the Spanish had not yet reached Upper California and that the Coast Miwok Indians would be happy to cede their land to Queen Elizabeth.

Drake named the land Nova Albion, presumably after the ancient name of England, Albion. The sea captain was also paying homage to the Elizabethan philosopher, mathematician, and historian John Dee, who wrote tales about England as the mystical realm of Albion. Before setting off on his voyage around the world, Drake secretly conferred with Dee, who gave him a description of Fernando Magellan's 1521 voyage around the tip of South America to the Pacific.

Drake's New Albion was almost as fantastical as Dee's. Joined at the hip to Mexico, California would always remain more Mediterranean than English.

San Francisco Begins in Tents

The City of San Francisco began as a stretch of tents along a windy cove on the western shore of the bay. The territory belonged to Mexico, and included a *presidio* or military post built by Spain on the site in 1776. This district is still known as the Presidio. The same year, Franciscan monks established a mission church two-and-a-half miles southwest of the cove. Mission Dolores remains the oldest building in San Francisco. In 1835, Captain William A. Richardson, an appointee of the Mexican government, pitched a tent on the site that is now Clay and Grant Streets and named the settlement Yerba Buena, or "good grass." In 1846, the U.S. wrested the territory from Mexico. Six months later, on January 30, 1847, it was renamed San Francisco, after Saint Francis of Assisi and Sebastián Cermeño's original naming.

The Golden Gate

Army scout John C. Frémont coined the term "Golden Gate" when he saw that the San Francisco harbor afforded great advantages for commerce with Asia. In a speech to Congress in 1847, Frémont named the bay's entrance "*Chrysopylae* (golden gate)… on the same principle that the harbor of Byzantium (Constantinople)… was called *Chrysoceras* (golden horn)." Constantinople's harbor was dubbed the Golden Horn because it brought the riches of the east to the capitol. Likewise the Golden Gate provided an ideal water route for trade between the U.S. and Asia.

At the time of Frémont's speech, high officials in Washington, D.C. also knew about California's gold-rich soil. Most history books claim the date for the discovery of gold as January 24, 1848—nine days before the U.S. claimed California in the Treaty of Guadalupe Hidalgo. But evidence suggests that the U.S. government knew about the gold in California in early 1846, before declaring war on Mexico. They simply kept quiet about it until California became U.S. territory.

San Francisco: The Mormon Promised Land?

San Francisco, the modern-day Babylon, almost became the virtuous capitol of the Church of Latter Day Saints. On February 15, 1846—the same day that Brigham Young led his flock out of Nauvoo, Illinois, toward the promised land of Salt Lake City, Utah—Samuel Brannan, a Mormon Elder, left the New York harbor with 220 Mormons aboard the ship *Brooklyn*. He headed for the West Coast hoping to found a new nation. But before the ship reached California, the U.S. defeated Mexico. On July 9, 1846, Captain John B. Montgomery landed his warship *Portsmouth* at what is now Portsmouth Square and planted the Stars and

Stripes on the Presidio, claiming California for the U.S. When Brannan sailed through the Golden Gate several days later, the first thing he saw was the U.S. flag. Legend has it Brannan threw down his hat and yelled, "There's that damned rag again!"

Low on supplies, the Mormons anchored and pitched their tents on shore. Seeing the advantages of the mild climate and fertile soil, Brannan raced overland and urged Brigham Young to build the Mormon State around the San Francisco Bay rather than the Great Salt Lake. Young refused, fearing that the Mormons would face too much competition from other settlers.

Brannan returned to the bay and persuaded his band of Mormons to settle there.

Brannan sadly returned to the bay and persuaded his band of Mormons to settle there. In January 1847, he launched the *California Star*, San Francisco's first newspaper. Legend has it that when James Marshall found gold, Brannan ran through Portsmouth Square shouting, "Gold on the American River!"—but only after he cornered the market on picks and axes. As the San Francisco Mormons amassed fortunes, Brigham Young demanded "the Lord's share." Brannan replied that he would pay when the Lord himself signed the order. After Brannan left the Mormon Church, he continued to play a prominent role in gold rush San Francisco. In 1851, he organized the first Vigilance Committee to improve law and order in the city. Despite his pick-ax monopoly, Brannan died penniless. His wife divorced him and took all his money.

Native Gold

Some people wonder why the California Indians, who had lived in northern California for at least 10,000 years, didn't discover the gold in their soil long before the Anglo-American settlers. In fact, the indigenous tribes of northern California knew about gold, but never bothered to collect it. Gold had no value in their cultures. The native peoples used the shells of the dentalium mollusk as a form of currency and a token of wealth. They also valued obsidian and used it to make arrowheads and knives for hunting and ceremonial use.

A City Built on Ships

San Francisco sits on a small sliver of land surrounded by water. The city officially covers 129 square miles, but only 47 square miles of this is solid earth. The other 82 square miles lie in the ocean and the bay.

The city's first landfill was unintentional. The financial district rests upon the skeletons of ships abandoned during the gold rush. The moment a vessel docked in the port, passengers and crew would take off for the gold mines, leaving their ship to rot. In 1849, Yerba Buena cove harbored 600 abandoned ships. They fell apart in "Rotten Row" and eventually became landfill.

Some citizens dragged the ships onto the beach and converted them into buildings. The hulk of the *General Harrison* became the Yank Sing restaurant. The *Euphemia* became a prison and an insane asylum.

Construction companies still find the ships and their forgotten cargo when they dig below the surface of the downtown. In 1976, three cases of century-old champagne turned up in hold of an abandoned ship called the *Niantic*.

The Population Explosion

San Francisco's population grew from 200 to 420 in 1846. By 1848, it had risen to 900. By 1850—one year after the gold rush started—35,000 people lived in San Francisco, and most of them were adult men under 40. From 1860 to 1870, the population jumped again from 57,000 to 149,000. In 1900, San Francisco had 343,000 residents and was the nation's eighth largest city.

A Boomtown Economy

At the beginning of the gold rush, real estate prices skyrocketed. One lot next to Portsmouth Square sold for $16.50 in 1847, $6,000 in early 1848, and $45,000 later that same year.

Meanwhile, there weren't nearly enough places to sleep. Enterprising San Franciscans rented bunks without mattresses or springs for $15 a night. When they ran out of bunks, they leased benches, tabletops, and even rocking chairs.

One desperate man rented a hole in the ground for $250 a month. Most of these places were so filthy that the sleeping miners had to cover their heads so rats wouldn't gnaw their noses or ears. Laundry cost even more than sleeping space. The standard price was $20 for 12 pieces of clothing.

In 1849, the miners excavated 40 million dollars worth of gold from the land north-east of San Francisco, in the Sierra Nevada. The cost of living was so high that they squandered most of this newfound wealth. Men who had never earned more than living wage frittered away their fortunes on gambling, booze, and harlots, as well as outrageously priced food and lodging. The soil was so rich with gold, and the miners so profligate, that one could find a few ounces of gold by panning the dust on the floor of the local saloons, gambling houses, and brothels. In *The Gold Hunters*, J. D. Borthwick described how "laboring men fastened their coarse, dirty shirts with a cluster of diamonds the size of a shilling." Many had all their teeth pulled and replaced with solid gold dentures. Dr. Henry Cogswell, the first California doctor to use chloroform as an anesthetic, made a fortune installing gold crowns and donated numerous water fountains to the city. Most of the fountains included monuments of Cogswell himself—a temperance advocate—magnanimously offering a glass of water to a thirsty pedestrian.

A correspondent for the *New York Evening Post* checked out the scene in late 1849 and recorded in his journal that "the people of San Francisco are mad, stark mad."

A Pinch of Gold

During the gold rush, people used gold as currency. A drink might cost a "pinch of gold"—as much gold dust as you could pick up between your thumb and forefinger. To maximize their profits, saloons hired the waiters with the largest fingertips. At the time, a pinch of gold equaled a dollar. The same pinch is now worth $20 to $25.

City of Bachelors

The gold rush transformed San Francisco from a tiny hamlet into an almost exclusively male boomtown. During the first year, the men outnumbered the women a hundred to one—probably the greatest peacetime gender imbalance in history. In a letter dated 1849, Colonel James J. Ayer wrote, "Ladies are an unknown quantity in this heterogeneous population."

The miners had same-sex dances, where some of the men dressed as women and danced with the other men. When a woman walked down the street, business stopped and a crowd of men trailed her, trying to protect her from each other. Once, during a property auction on Montgomery Street, a man stepped into the auction room and announced, "Two ladies going by on the sidewalk!" The crowd immediately ran outside.

The Founding Mothers

For the first year of the gold rush, fewer than 300 women lived in San Francisco. Two hundred were Mexican, Peruvian, and Chilean prostitutes, who camped in tents and shanties along the waterfront at Broadway and Pacific on the eastern and southern sides of Telegraph Hill. In some cases, six women shared one unfurnished tent and entertained several clients at the same time.

During the first half of 1850, roughly 2,000 prostitutes migrated to San Francisco from the French demimonde and from the underworlds of New York and New Orleans. The newspapers informed readers of new female arrivals and their availability. Many of these women amassed fortunes, and the more elegant prostitutes became powerful socialites. From the gold rush through the turn of the century, the city's economic development pivoted upon the sex trade. San Francisco's first women entrepreneurs were prostitutes, and the madams often made more money than their gold-digging clientele.

Politicians on Horseback

Early politicians in San Francisco attracted voters with their excellent riding skills. When San Francisco's first election took place in 1850, several colorful locals competed for office. Colonel J. J. Bryant, a Democrat, ran for sheriff against Colonel John E. Townes, a Whig who had previously been appointed sheriff. Colonel Jack Hayes, a Texas Ranger, ran as an independent candidate. Bryant, a gambling-house owner, decorated his hotel with flags and banners, hired a band to play patriotic ditties, and served free food and drinks. But Hayes won by a landslide by appearing on election day astride a black stallion and exhibiting what the *Annals of San Francisco* called "some of the finest specimens of horsemanship ever witnessed."

The Fatal Black Pearl

Adelaide Nielsen, a popular actress, made her San Francisco stage debut in 1874 as Juliet. In 1880, Nielsen gave her last performance at the Baldwin Theater and prepared to continue her career in Europe. Before leaving, she offered theater owner David Belasco a gem from her jewelery box as a parting gift. Belasco chose a black pearl. Nielsen said she couldn't part with the pearl, which was her good luck charm. If she gave it up, she would die. Later the actress reconsidered and sent Belasco the pearl. She died in Paris only four weeks later.

Mary Ellen Pleasant—Saint or Vixen?

Mary Ellen Pleasant was a controversial woman. During her life in San Francisco, she won considerable notoriety as a blackmailer, extortionist, voodoo queen, murderess, and a "woman of mystery whose deeds are evil," as one newspaper put it. People spread strange, malicious rumors, blaming Pleasant for more than a dozen deaths. Tales circulated that Pleasant held voodoo rituals with wild dancing, drumming, and snake worship at her cottage in Geneva, south of San Francisco. The city's elite supposedly paid $500 a head to attend these wild, uninhibited gatherings.

Though it's hard to separate fact from fiction, Pleasant was most likely the victim of rumors spread by people who didn't understand her religion (Haitian voodoo) and couldn't fathom how a black woman could befriend the city's elite without practicing black magic. Pleasant studied voodoo in New Orleans with Marie Laveau, a famous voodoo queen. Though voodoo is the main religion in Haiti, many Americans, then as now, equate it with black magic and superstition.

This controversial women is commemorated in a plaque on the sidewalk at 1661 Octavia Street that reads: Mary Ellen Pleasant (1814–1904), the "Mother of Civil Rights in California." The daughter of a Haitian-born voodoo priestess and the son of a Virginia governor, Mary was born a slave in antebellum Georgia. Like other slaves, she was given only a first name. While Mary was still a child, a wealthy man recognized her intelligence and bought her out of slavery. It was illegal to teach black people to read and write, but Mary—with light skin, one brown eye, and one blue eye—passed as white to gain an education and avoid being forced back into slavery.

Later in life, she preferred to reveal her real heritage. After Lincoln issued the Emancipation Proclamation in 1863, she chose to list her name as "Mary

E. Pleasant, colored" in the *San Francisco Directory*. Although the white inhabitants of San Francisco called her by the nickname of "Mammy" Pleasant, she reportedly hated this name.

When she came to San Francisco in April 1852, Pleasant had already guided numerous slaves to freedom through the Underground Railroad. Having inherited her first husband's fortune, she backed abolitionist causes, including John Brown's raid on Harper's Ferry. Pleasant also sued the city of San Francisco after she was thrown off a streetcar because of her color.

The case went all the way to the California Supreme Court, and in 1868 she won the right for blacks to ride in San Francisco trolley cars. She thus anticipated Rosa Parks by 83 years and set a precedent for civil rights legislation of the 1960s.

In 1868, she won the right for blacks to ride in trolley cars.

Pleasant also invested her inheritance wisely and became one of the wealthiest women in the nation. With her secret business partner Thomas Bell, she amassed a joint fortune of $30 million.

Pleasant was certainly a pioneer of civil rights and probably also a shrewd manipulator and con artist, based on the little that's known of her life. She wrote memoirs, but was known for exaggerating her own story. San Francisco called her "The Black City Hall" because she sheltered escaped slaves and found them jobs in the homes of prominent citizens. She knew all the civic leaders and had spies in many of their households. In exchange for her favors, the former slaves told Pleasant their bosses' secrets. She supposedly made quite a profit by keeping quiet.

Pleasant made similar deals with young women from poor backgrounds. When Pleasant arrived in San Francisco, the male-to-female ratio was six to one, and marriageable young ladies were in high demand. Pleasant would take a working-class girl under her wing, teach her etiquette, grooming, and proper English, and then marry her off to a wealthy businessman. The protégée thanked Pleasant with funds from her new husband's bank account and kept her abreast of his business secrets as well.

Move Chinatown?

While Mayor Eugene Schmitz was in office, he and boss Abe Ruef tried to scare the Chinese out of Chinatown. After the 1906 earthquake destroyed the district, they wanted to move San Francisco's Chinese population to Hunters Point. But China's Empress Cixi sent her deputy ambassador in Washington D.C. to San Francisco to pressure city leaders into letting the Chinese rebuild the nation's largest Chinatown at its current location.

KGB Opens Office in San Francisco

In December 1941, the KGB opened a covert office in San Francisco. KGB communications referred to the local director, Grigory Kheifitz, as Charon (*Kharon* in Russian), after the boatman in Etruscan and Greek mythology who ferried the dead across the river Styx. California was "Charon's shore." Washington, D.C. was code-named "Carthage" and New York "Tyre." San Francisco was, of course, "Babylon." Kheifitz oversaw the capture of numerous soviet mariners trying to jump ship in San Francisco and sent them back to the USSR for imprisonment or immediate execution.

Newspaper Editor Kidnapped

Fremont Older was managing editor of the San Francisco *Bulletin* and a political reformer. When San Francisco voters reelected the corrupt Mayor Eugene Schmitz in 1905, Older launched a graft investigation with the help of Theodore Roosevelt and the financial support of Rudolph Spreckels, son of a California sugar baron. Mayor Schmitz and boss Abe Ruef were convicted of extortion, and numerous prominent San Franciscans faced corruption charges.

In 1907, an attorney and a detective hired by Ruef's accomplice, Patrick Calhoun, kidnapped Older on Van Ness Avenue using a phony arrest warrant. The kidnappers were holding Older captive aboard a southbound Southern

Pacific train when a fellow passenger, a lawyer, heard them talk menancingly about taking Older for "a run through the mountains." The lawyer telephoned San Francisco, and police boarded the train and rescued Older in Santa Barbara.

Once Ruef was in prison, Older changed his mind about the corruption in San Francisco. Deciding the system—not Ruef—was the problem, Older visited Ruef in prison and campaigned for his release.

Native Becomes Museum Attraction

On September 4, 1911, Alfred L. Kroeber, who founded the University of California at Berkeley's anthropology department and the field of California Indian ethnography, took Ishi, a northern California Indian, to live in the university's anthropology museum in San Francisco.

The Indian had been found starving and frightened outside a slaughterhouse near Oroville. As far as anyone knew, he had lost his entire family and tribe. He moved into the museum, where he taught Kroeber to speak his native tongue and showed audiences how he made arrow points and built fires. People treated Ishi like a living museum piece. Ishi was generous, and even though white settlers had slaughtered his people, he was eager to help the anthropologists record his language and culture. Kroeber thought Ishi was the last of the Yahi—a subgroup of the Yana Indians killed by white bounty hunters. For nearly a century, California schoolchildren learned that Ishi was a real-life last of the

Mohicans—the last "wild Indian" to survive the white settlers' massacre of indigenous tribes.

Then, in 1997, Ishi's nearest kin came forth to claim his remains. Under repatriation laws, anthropologists and museums must return Native American cultural and material remains to the tribes to whom they belonged. Four Maidu Indian tribes from Butte County requested Ishi's ashes, which they wanted to bury on Yahi ground. They'd heard that Ishi's brain had been removed during autopsy. In May 1999, the Smithsonian agreed to return the 83-year-old brain to Ishi's relatives, the Redding Rancheria and Pit River tribes in Butte County.

The discovery of the missing brain raised questions about Kroeber's ethics. Berkeley anthropologist Jonathan Marks asked how Kroeber could objectify Ishi, whom he considered a friend and "add a pickled Indian brain to his macabre collections." Kroeber's student and colleague George M. Foster explained that the late anthropologist was in Europe when Ishi died. He sent a letter forbidding autopsy, but it was too late. Kroeber spent six months trying to figure out what to do with the "bottled brain of a close friend in his office."

As it turns out, Ishi probably wasn't full-blooded Yahi, nor was he the last of his kind. Ishi never even revealed his name to Kroeber. According to Native American custom, he may have considered it dangerous to tell strangers his name. When news reporters pressured Kroeber to reveal the Indian's name, the anthropologist said "Ishi," meaning "man" in Yana.

The Yellow Peril

Around 1917, William Randolph Hearst's *San Francisco Examiner* spread rumors that Japan was invading California. The stories terrified residents and sales of newspapers rocketed. The state took the warnings to heart and spent more than a million dollars fortifying the California coast, installing cannons from Eureka to Monterey. The Japanese invaded Pearl Harbor many years later. The cannons remain in place today.

No city invites the heart to come to life as San Francisco does. Arrival in San Francisco is an experience in living.

— William Saroyan

The Downfall of Fatty Arbuckle

Comedian Roscoe "Fatty" Arbuckle was a silent film star, second only to Charlie Chaplin in fame. On September 5, 1921, Arbuckle threw a party in suites 1219, 1220, and 1221 of the St. Francis Hotel at 335 Powell Street in Union Square. During the party, actress Virginia Rappe got sick. The guests believed she was drunk, but actually her bladder had ruptured. On September 9, Rappe died of peritonitis. No one knows what caused the peritonitis, because several of her organs were missing after the autopsy. Some speculate that Rappe died from a botched abortion, and the physician who performed the illegal abortion had her organs removed to protect himself.

After Rappe's death, rumors spread that Arbuckle had raped her during the party. He was charged with murder and only absolved after three trials—the scandal had ruined his career. Arbuckle died penniless, while Rappe achieved notoriety as a ghost at the Moss Beach Distillery on Highway 1, south of the city.

The Mud Plague

During the winter of 1849–1850, mud plagued San Francisco. After 50 inches of rain, the town's few dirt roads turned into mud-holes. People sank knee-deep. City authorities dumped cartfuls of brushwood into the streets to make them passable, but the fill quickly vanished. The mud consumed wagons, carts, several animals, and even a few drunks who tried to cross the street and drowned. Their bodies weren't found until weeks later. As far as we know, the mud plague has no connection to the "mud people," who ran through the financial district in the 1990s naked, grunting, and covered in mud.

Fire Consumes Two-Thirds of the City

Mother Nature sometimes unleashes her fury on San Francisco. At 5:12 A.M. on Wednesday, April 18, 1906, an earthquake measuring between 7.7 and 8.3 on the

Richter scale struck the city. Fires broke out across town as gas mains cracked and chimneys collapsed. The flames merged into one enormous blaze, reaching 2,700 degrees Fahrenheit. In three days it devoured 2,593 acres, roughly two-thirds of the city. By the time it burned out, the statistics were devastating—250,000 people were homeless, and an estimated 700 were dead or missing. In the 1980s, revised estimates claimed 3,000 died as a result of the quake and fire.

The year before the blaze, the National Association of Fire Underwriters had evaluated San Francisco's fire-preparedness and issued a report stating that the fire department was drastically underequipped and understaffed, and the city had "violated all precedents by not burning up." The Board of Supervisors ignored the report. During the earthquake, Fire Chief Dennis Sullivan, who had spent years pleading for a larger staff and better facilities, was killed in the fire station by falling bricks.

The fire following the 1906 quake raged for days. Families who had lost their homes swarmed into Golden Gate Park. The mayor had to call in the army, which stopped the influx of looters, imposed a curfew, and shot people returning to the wreckage. Survivors dodged bullets as they tried to rescue family and friends trapped in the rubble. Trapped victims burned alive as the flames swept over them.

The earthquake ruptured water lines, making most hydrants inoperable. Failing to quench the fire with water, city officials decided to create a giant firebreak.

They seized two blocks of buildings on either side of Van Ness Avenue and dynamited them to the ground. This swath of destruction stopped the fire from burning west all the way to the ocean. The tactic also saved the Victorian houses of Haight-Ashbury and other neighborhoods west of Van Ness.

The San Francisco Fire Department commemorates the earthquake each year on April 18 at 5 A.M. by serving free Bloody Marys and Screwdrivers at Lotta's Fountain at Market, Kearney, and Third streets.

Bubonic Plague

The bubonic plague broke out in San Francisco in 1900 and again in 1907. Fearing that the news would hurt the economy, city officials kept the first outbreak secret. In the Chinatown district, 113 people died. In 1907, 160 people fell ill and 77 died. The city launched a public rat hunt and began inspecting buildings, ripping up floorboards, and testing 150,000 rodents for the disease. Historical records are not clear as to the fate of the rodents.

> The city launched a public rat hunt, inspecting buildings, ripping up floorboards, and testing 150,000 rodents.

Earthquake Panic

On May 21, 1996, when an earthquake of 4.7 shook San Francisco, 21-year-old Eduardo Meneses thought someone was breaking into his house. Grabbing his gun, he raced upstairs and shot himself in the leg.

Bridge Over Troubled Waters

On a clear day, the Golden Gate Bridge offers a panoramic view of the bay and the San Francisco skyline. "What Nature rent asunder long ago man has joined today," said chief engineer Joseph Strauss at the bridge's opening ceremony in May 1937. But not everyone who crosses its span sees cause for optimism and faith in humanity. The 1.2-mile bridge is the world's most popular suicide site. Roughly every two weeks, someone climbs the four-foot railing and plunges to an almost certain death.

"Jumping from the bridge is seen as sure, quick, clean, and available," says Dr. Jerome Motto, a Bay Area suicide expert. "It's like having a loaded gun on your kitchen table." At low tide, the bridge is 222 feet from the bay's surface—the same height as a 19-story building. The drop takes four seconds. Dr. Lanny Berman, the executive director of the American Association of Suicidology, says, "Jumpers are drawn to the Golden Gate because they believe it's a gateway to another place. They think that life will slow down in those final seconds, and then they'll hit the water cleanly, like a high diver."

Most people who jump off the Golden Gate Bridge die instantly, hitting the surface of the water at 75 miles per hour. Ribs break, puncturing the heart. Others drown, sometimes plunging 350 feet to the bottom of the bay. The death toll has passed 1,200—and that's only the people who have been seen leaping or pulled out of the icy water. "The rare survivors always hit feet first, and at a slight angle," writes Tad Friend, reporting for *The New Yorker*.

Only 26 people have survived. Many say they regretted their decision immediately. "I still see my hands coming off the railing," says Ken Baldwin, who jumped in 1985. "I instantly realized that everything in my life that I'd thought was unfixable was totally fixable—except for having just jumped."

Suicide barriers have virtually eliminated leaps from the Eiffel Tower, Empire State Building, St. Peter's Basilica, and other common suicide sites. But San Franciscans have resisted proposals for a Golden Gate suicide barrier, even though their most common fear is gephyrophobia, the dread of crossing bridges. Some people think that a barrier would be futile, because those who want to kill themselves will find some other way to do it.

This is not actually the case, says Dr. Richard Seiden, Berkeley professor and foremost researcher on suicide at the Golden Gate. In a study called "Where Are They Now?" Seiden followed up on more than 500 people who were deterred from jumping off the bridge between 1937 and 1971. Ninety-four percent of these potential suicides were still living and had not transferred their tendencies to fast-moving trains, trucks, or mending electrical equipment in the bath.

Suicide Cult Leads Anti-Suicide March

The Reverend Jim Jones, who later led a mass suicide of his followers in Jonestown, Guyana, ironically led an anti-suicide march on the Golden Gate Bridge. During the 1977 rally, he called the Golden Gate "a symbol of human ingenuity, technological genius, but social failure." The rally, which took place on Memorial Day, included 600 of Jones' followers from The People's Temple cult. The protesters demanded the installation of suicide barriers to prevent the despairing from flinging themselves off the bridge. Jones gave a speech at the event in which he mentioned, "I have been in a suicidal mood myself today for perhaps the first time in my life." The mass suicide at Jonestown took place 18 months later.

Keeping Score of Suicides

Until the mid 1990s, every time someone leaped off the Golden Gate Bridge, the *San Francisco Chronicle* and *Examiner* printed the cumulative number. In 1973, when both papers began the count to number 500, bridge personnel stopped 14 prospective jumpers, including a man wearing the number "500" pinned to his shirt. Hoping to discourage copycats, suicide prevention activists pressured the newspapers to stop the hype. The papers finally halted the count in 1995, when the number passed 1,000. Now they only cover celebrity jumps and people who block traffic. Perhaps this explains why people tend to throw themselves off the east side of the bridge—not only because it's a better view, but because they drive onto the bridge from San Francisco rather than bucolic suburban Marin.

Even animals are tempted by the lure of the Golden Gate. When a dog jumped off the bridge in the early 1990s, the *Chronicle* ran the headline "Dog Suicide" and published a map tracing the canine's final walk through the city.

You are fortunate to live here. If I were your President, I would levy a tax on you for living in San Francisco!

— Mikhail Gorbachev

Monkey See, Monkey Do

In the 1970s, Tallulah the chimp broke out of her cage at the San Francisco Zoo and raided the snack bar. As she stuffed her face with food, a guard with a gun arrived on the scene. In a classic silver screen maneuver, Tallulah snatched the gun out of his hands and aimed it at him, holding the guard hostage until a zookeeper came to the rescue.

Penguin Abduction

In 1987, a homeless man named Skippy kidnapped penguin No. 102 from the San Francisco Zoo. The police nabbed Skippy on Ocean Beach, but as they were handcuffing him, they got an emergency call and had to zip over to the Richmond district to catch an ax murderer. Skippy escaped, and penguin No. 102 got to ride in the back of the squad car for hours, watching the police in action. Weeks later, another abducted penguin showed up at the Haight district's firehouse.

Chaos at Penguin Island

On Christmas Eve 2002, 52 Magellanic penguins embarked on a "Great Migration" in the 130-by-40-foot pool at the San Francisco Zoo. In the wild, Magellanic penguins take off from Patagonia every winter and swim about 1,500 miles north to Brazil. Raised in captivity, the birds at the zoo's "Penguin Island" had forgotten their ancestral ways. They spent every winter lounging in their burrows—until six new penguins from the Ohio Sea World jump-started their migratory patterns.

The newcomers, perhaps confused by their long journey, hurled themselves into the pool and swam in furious circles. You might think the lazy San Francisco birds would look down on this absurd behavior. But within two hours, all 52 penguins were "whirling around the pool like tuxedos in a washing machine." For more than two months, they swam all day at breakneck speed, barely staggering out of the water at night to sleep. When the zookeepers drained the pool, the penguins waddled around in circles in the empty tub.

Jane Tollini, the penguin keeper, didn't know what to make of her normally fat, sluggish charges. They barely stopped to eat, and some of them looked as if they'd gone on the Dexatrim diet. Visitors came up with bizarre theories to explain the sudden pointless migration. Some said the penguins were warning us of a coming Ice Age. Others suggested that electromagnetic fields in the water were disturbing their brain chemistry. No one knew when the frenzy would stop.

> *Some said the penguins were warning us of an Ice Age.*

Mating season finally put an end to the frantic swimming. In March, the birds climbed out of the pool and began preening each other. The next winter, they returned to their languid ways.

Rowdy Teens Sent to San Francisco Zoo

In September 2004, two teenage female grizzly bears ransacked a ranch outside Augusta, Montana. First, they broke into the calving shed and wolfed down 150 pounds of corn. "They just raised havoc," said Terri Tew, the ranch's owner. "They flung things around, chewed on a 4-H banner, flattened a plastic garbage can." Several weeks later, they pillaged the barn and front yard—pulling up carrots, stomping on bird feeders, and devouring Tew's oat crop. "They pooped all over the place," said the rancher, who finally captured the girls with the help of a game warden.

The bears, who turned out to be sisters, arrived at their new home, the San Francisco Zoo, in October. The two are the first grizzlies there since 1989. "They are very attractive bears," said Michael Madel, a biologist who helped capture the sisters. "I've been working with bears for 25 years and these are two of the nicest-looking bears I've ever seen." They were 18 months old when captured, adolescents in bear years. One is chocolate brown and one is blond.

Old Lady Foils Laptop Thieves

In the Haight-Ashbury district, a gang of thieves was snatching laptop computers from people walking down the street or sitting at outdoor cafes. Then one day, an elderly woman stormed into a local cafe. Gesturing angrily with her cane, she declared that she had had enough of crime and was going to fight back. Onlookers wondered what she'd do, as she ambled away in a huff. Several days later, the woman sat down at an outdoor cafe and began typing on a battered laptop. As it turned out, the computer was broken. She was using it as a decoy to lure the thieves.

The lady returned to the cafe every day for several weeks and pretended to type. People chatted with her; the cafe owners bought her free cups of tea. One day, she finally lured her quarry. A young man walked by her table and grabbed the laptop.

But as he turned to run, the woman smacked him sharply with her cane. The laptop, which was secretly chained to the cafe table, flew out of the man's hands and clattered on the sidewalk. Cafe patrons leaped on the thief and turned him over to the police. The lady has become a neighborhood hero.

Typo Creates Telephone Havoc

On June 26, 1992, San Francisco and four other major cities suffered a massive breakdown in telephone service, affecting 12 million anxious customers. In a November report, DSC Communications traced the disruption to a DSC keyboard technician who entered the wrong computer code, accidentally typing a "6" rather than a "d."

Consumer Advisor Receives Odd Complaints

San Jose Mercury News "Action Line" columnist Dennis Rockstroh has helped San Francisco Bay Area consumers slice through red tape, lodge complaints, and secure refunds from stubborn retail stores for the last 30 years. The columnist sometimes receives odd complaints and questions, including the following from 1991:

"I voted for the Lotto game eight years ago, and I haven't won anything. I think some of these people who are winning these millions of dollars didn't even vote for the program."

"During the time I've been in the main jail, my sexual feeling/response has rapidly declined to almost non-existent. I'm 25 and have never experienced such a severe lack of sexual drive."

"Do people with big noses produce bigger boogers than people with smaller noses?"

Mormon Gunmen Battle in Desert

When the gold rush struck, Brigham Young, the founder of the Church of Jesus Christ of Latter Day Saints, demanded "the Lord's share" from Samuel Brannan and the other Mormons who settled in San Francisco. When Brannan refused, Young sent his posse, known as the Destroying Angels, to collect. But Brannan had his own bodyguards, the Exterminators, who met the Angels in the desert and drove them off.

Inventor of Television Won't Let His Kids Watch It

Philo Taylor Farnsworth, the inventor of television, came up with the idea while tilling a potato field at age 14. He imagined an electronic beam scanning the images back and forth in the same way he was plowing the field (or in the same way one reads a book). The boy drew a picture and gave it to his chemistry teacher, Justin Tolman. In 1927, Farnsworth assembled his "Image Dissector" at a laboratory at 202 Green Street, San Francisco. He was just 21.

Unfortunately, Farnsworth spent much of his adult life battling the Radio Corporation of America (RCA), which refused to pay him royalties. During the trials, Tolman, the chemistry teacher, testified that Farnsworth had conceived of the television in high school. He even produced the drawing of the electronic tube that Farnsworth had sketched at age 14. The drawing looked almost like the Image Dissector patented eight years later.

After years of litigations, RCA agreed to pay Farnsworth royalties, but by that time the corporation only had to pay him for a few years before his patents expired. As soon as they did, RCA launched a major PR campaign, promoting the chief of RCA as the inventor of television.

Farnsworth suffered from depression and alcoholism. He received electric shock therapy, and in 1947, his house burned down. In 1957, the TV show *What's My Line?* invited him to appear as a mystery guest. Referring to Farnsworth as Dr. X, the host asked the panel to guess what this man had done to earn his place on the show. One panelist asked Dr. X whether he had invented a machine that could cause pain. Farnsworth replied, "Yes. Sometimes it's most painful."

Finally, even though Farnsworth invented television, he didn't want his children watching it. His son Kent said, "Throughout my childhood his reaction to television was 'There's nothing on it worthwhile, and we're not going to watch it in this household, and I don't want it in your intellectual diet.'"

Strange San Francisco Laws

San Francisco has a number of bizarre laws that remain in place today:

• A city ordinance prohibits any "mechanical device that reproduces obscene language."
• In a car wash, one may not wipe off a car with used underwear.
• Stink balls and kerchoo powders are illegal.
• One may not beat a rug in front of a house.
• A city ordinance bans "cane games." Municipal authorities have no clue what cane games are, but they decided not to take the law off the books, in case some day cane games reappear and the city needs a law against them.

Prosecutor Survives Point Blank Shot to the Head

Federal attorney Francis J. Heney prosecuted Mayor Eugene Schmitz and Abe Ruef in one of the most sensational trials in San Francisco history. Ruef had the city in his pocket. He secured the mayor's elections, wrote his speeches, and extorted bribes from utilities, businesses, and the Board of Supervisors—and he wasn't about to let a graft prosecution stop him.

When Ruef stood trial, he tried to bribe prospective jurors and place his cronies on the panel. Heney examined 1,450 prospective jurors before he could select a jury that was as unbiased as possible.

During the trial, Heney was speaking with one of his assistants in the courtroom when Morris Haas, a juror whom Heney had dismissed, walked up to the prosecutor's table, drew a gun, and shot Heney point blank in the right ear. Witnesses assumed Heney was dead, but the bullet missed his brain and lodged in the muscles of his left jaw. He survived with his voice and speaking abilities still intact.

Haas and Ruef were thrown in jail. Many suspected Ruef was behind the shooting. That night, Haas was found dead in his cell. Two weeks later, police chief William J. Biggy, who may have shot Haas, vanished on November 30, 1908. He was later found floating in the bay on December 15.

The Saga of Constance May Flood

When San Francisco multimillionaire James L. Flood died in February 1926, friends of the family were surprised that the obituary failed to mention Constance—James's daughter by his first wife, Rose, who had died when Constance was only five.

Around 1893, Rose had written to her family that she was expecting a baby. Months later, another letter announced that the baby was a girl, Constance May. San Francisco newspapers of the 1890s contained numerous references to Constance May Flood. Shortly after Rose died, Jim married his wife's sister, Maud. After that, no one heard anything more about Constance. People made inquiries. Finally, a journalist contacted the lawyer handling Flood's estate. The lawyer said James Flood never had a daughter named Constance.

In August 1926, Mrs. John P. Gavin, formerly Constance May Flood, came forth to claim her inheritance. She told the press that her father and her Aunt Maud had sent her to live in a convent. She wrote to her father every week, but never heard anything back. James Flood's personal secretary told her she was not the daughter of Mr. Flood and his first wife, but a "waif that Mrs. Flood took into her home" and kept until she died.

At the hearing, the Floods' friends, neighbors, and servants testified that

Constance May had been the daughter of Jim and Rose Flood. They spoke of Jim's demonstrative love for Constance, how he spoke of her as "my darling daughter," and even had the gardener plant flowers spelling out the name Constance on the estate.

Then a drawn-faced woman named Eudora Willette took the stand and claimed she was Constance's mother. She had had an affair with Jim Flood in 1892, when Jim's wife Rose was in Europe. The Floods and their lawyers, as well as Constance and her lawyers, accepted that Mrs. Willette was her mother. In a face-to-face meeting, Mrs. Willette swore to Constance that James Flood was her biological father.

But several years later, Mrs. Willette's testimony changed. She arrived at a deposition by limosine sporting fashionable clothes, makeup, and an extravagant hairdo. When the Floods' attorney asked, "Who was the father of Constance?" she replied, "James Cannon." Some speculated that the Floods had paid Mrs. Willette off.

In July 1931, the case went to trial. Despite a strong popular bias toward Mrs. Gavin, Judge George H. Buck ordered the jury to arrive at the following verdict: James L. Flood was not the father of Constance May Gavin. The courtroom hissed. The jurors objected, but when one juror was found in contempt of court, the others obeyed the judge. While still in the courtroom, the jurors voted 10 to two that James Flood was Constance's father. The public was furious. The State

Supreme Court ruled that Buck had erred and ordered a retrial. But the Floods negotiated a settlement, giving Constance one million dollars.

Constance died at the age of 56. A widow with no children, she willed her estate to charity. The will specifically disinherited Mrs. Willette, who sued nonetheless. The court awarded Mrs. Willette $78,000 from Constance's estate.

Surgeons Rush to Save Celebrity Ape

Zoo gorillas usually see veterinarians instead of doctors for their health concerns. But in May 2004, a team of University of California, San Francisco surgeons left their usual duties carving up humans to perform a high-tech emergency procedure on Kubi, a 422-pound gorilla at the San Francisco Zoo. Kubi, the much-loved patriarch of the Gorilla World exhibit, had spent his entire life at the zoo and fathered three children. He was the younger brother of Koko, the "talking gorilla" who learned sign language. At age 29—roughly 60 in human terms—Kubi suffered from chronic lung ailments and was sure to die without medical intervention.

On the morning of May 7, a group of anesthesiologists and zoo workers zapped Kubi with tranquilizer darts and rushed him to the hospital. "He was a challenge to anesthetize, being a 400-pound gorilla," said Dr. Jacqueline Jencek, a zoo veterinarian. To remove Kubi's infected lung, "The surgeons had to make it through skin three times as thick as the average human's. All the breathing tubes and other instruments had to be super-sized."

"He's built for endurance," said Dr. David Jablons, one of the thoracic surgeons who operated on the ape. "Everything is kind of bigger, thicker, and tougher. But the anatomy was comparable."

The operation was the first open-chest surgery performed on a nonhuman primate. But despite antibiotics and get-well wishes, Kubi died of an infection several days after the procedure.

"Kubi was a tremendous spirit and he leaves a legacy as a gentle and sensitive individual," said Dr. Freeland Dunker, senior veterinarian. "Lessons learned from his life here at the zoo will be valuable to others for many years to come." Zoo workers, fans, and lady gorillas all miss the great ape, who "won countless hearts with his gentle demeanor and soulful gaze." During Kubi's 12-hour surgery, "The females made a stir back in Gorilla World, uttering loud distress calls to register their displeasure at the absence of their beloved mate." Kubi is survived by Bwang, his partner of 22 years, his sons, Shango, 15, and Barney, 10, a daughter Nneka, five, and numerous male and female admirers.

Why We Are Broke

After the Great 1906 Earthquake, most banks in San Francisco closed to deal with the damages. But Amadeo Peter (A.P.) Giannini, the founder of the Bank of

Italy, set up shop on the docks. Behind a desk made out of a wooden plank and two barrels, Giannini gave credit "on a face and a signature" to common people who needed to rebuild their homes and their lives. Before the 1900s, banks were for people with money and property, but not for working stiffs. Giannini pioneered the kind of banking we know today—with installment credit, such as auto loans, home mortgages, and credit cards. He is the reason why we are all so broke today!

The Night of the Purple Hand

On Halloween 1969, a crowd of activists gathered at the *San Francisco Examiner's* headquarters to protest the newspaper's anti-gay editorial policies. Some *Examiner* employees climbed onto the building's roof and dumped a barrel of purple ink on the angry mob. The undeterred protesters stamped purple handprints throughout downtown San Francisco, and the demonstration became known as "The Night of the Purple Hand."

PART II:
Law & Disorder

They were a wonderful set of burglars, the people who were running San Francisco when I first came to town in 1923. Wonderful because, if they were stealing, they were doing it with class and style.

— Sally Stanford

I always see about six scuffles a night when I come to San Francisco. That's one of the town's charms.

— Errol Flynn

Always a rebellious city, San Francisco has never completely yielded to the rule of the law. Residents have tolerated and even welcomed illegal and nefarious activities for many years. An example of this was "crimping," a practice by which waterfront bar owners supported the city's seaport economy by kidnapping sailors to man the cargo ships. One notorious crimp, Shanghai Kelly, built trap doors in the floor of his bar to dispatch drugged sailors onto waiting boats below.

Other outlaws did less for the local economy. Roving thugs, the Sydney Ducks robbed, murdered, and almost burned the city down when the winds were favorable. Black Bart, the gentleman robber, held up stagecoaches and placed flowery poems at the scene, describing his dastardly deeds. He was finally captured when detectives traced the laundry mark on a hanky he left behind.

Seeking to restore order, vigilantes formed Vigilance Committees and dispensed frontier justice by hanging thieves from the roof of their downtown headquarters. Soldier of fortune William Walker set out from the city to invade Mexico and Nicaragua unsuccessfully before being shot by a firing squad in Honduras.

Politicians passed laws against crime, but some were only intended to harass the city's growing Chinese population. These included the 1875 ban against opium smoking, the nation's first anti-drug law. The San Francisco Bay Area is now the center of the medical marijuana movement, which seeks to repeal federal laws against the possession and cultivation of cannabis by patients.

In the end, San Francisco's periodic anti-vice crusades backfired. They only helped to advertise the city as a den of forbidden pleasures and lawlessness. Tourists flocked to "Babylon by the Bay" to spend their money in brothels and racy dives such as the Dash Club, which featured female impersonators.

During Prohibition, the city's politicians brought in carloads of fine bourbon whiskey for delegates of the 1920 National Democratic Convention. Other political shenanigans were less successful. When a judge tried to fix the verdict in Constance May Flood's celebrated inheritance case, irate citizens demanded recall proceedings against him.

Overwhelmed, police failed and still fail to stop criminals. They never caught the "Zodiac," San Francisco's most notorious serial killer. The Manson family lived in San Francisco, but moved to Los Angeles to carry out their murderous rampage. San Francisco cult leader Jim Jones also left the city before forcing his followers to commit mass suicide in Guyana. And murderer Dan White, who gunned down Mayor George Moscone and City Supervisor Harvey Milk, got off with a light sentence, citing his junk food diet as proof of mental instability.

San Francisco—the city with the nation's most above-ground underground—has also served as a hideout for fugitives. Who's going to find them amid all the human wildlife? Patty Hearst, William Randolph Hearst's 19-year-old granddaughter, laid low in San Francisco after her abduction by the Symbionese Liberation Army. She later aided her captors in a bank holdup. During the 1960s, members of the radical Weather Underground group also took cover near San Francisco, hoping to avoid arrest after their bombing campaign. LSD advocate Timothy Leary changed his identity and smuggled himself out of the city after supporters sprang him from prison.

Notorious Crimps

Early San Francisco's economy depended on the cargo ships that entered the harbor, unloaded, and sailed away with new goods. But as soon as a vessel anchored, most of the sailors abandoned ship and raced to the gold mines. Someone needed to ensure that cargo ships left the city with a complete crew, in order to keep the economy afloat.

The business of providing ships with sailors was known as "crimping." Captains paid a hefty fee for a full crew, incentivizing many of the waterfront bar owners to work as crimps. They probably began as legitimate business people, but when the supply of sailors dwindled, the crimps resorted to desperate means. They would "recruit" a sailor by slipping snuff or a plug of tobacco into a customer's whisky. If that didn't work, opium, laudanum, or chloral hydrate did the trick. If the victim was still standing, the crimp whacked him over the head with a club, then put him in a boat and rowed him out to the ship. When the recruit awoke, he found himself on a cargo vessel, headed for a distant port.

It was bad enough to wake up and find yourself on a ship headed for Alaska or Mexico, but it was much worse to discover that your vessel was bound for faraway Shanghai. The verb *to shanghai*, which means "to kidnap a sailor for pay," originated in San Francisco. The *Alta California* newspaper was the first to use the word in this sense in late 1853.

Shanghai Kelly

The crimp who perfected the art of shanghaiing was a red-bearded Irishman called Shanghai Kelly. Kelly kept a bar at 33 Pacific Street, in a rickety cabin built on stilts so the tide could wash in underneath. Kelly worked with "runners" who rowed out to meet the ships as they sailed into the harbor. The runners were supposed to ask the captain and crew what provisions they needed for the trip back, but they also urged the sailors to come to Kelly's bar for free alcohol. While drinking at Kelly's bar, the unsuspecting seamen would be drugged and then sold to the captain of another ship. Often the first captain would end up paying Kelly to replace his lost sailors and so Kelly doubled his business.

Kelly had three trapdoors on the floor in front of his bar. He would engage a visitor in conversation and gradually maneuver him down the bar, until he was standing over a trapdoor. Meanwhile the bartender mixed a knockout concoction. If a wary customer insisted on mixing his own drinks, Kelly would throw his arm around him and offer him a cigar, which happened to be laced with opium. As the customer lost consciousness, Kelly opened the trapdoor and dropped his victim into a boat waiting below, then the runners would row him out to a ship in need of crewmen.

If the victim died from the drug or the fall, the runners simply wrapped him in blankets and sold him to the captain anyway. Since most sailors were unconscious when the runners carried them onboard, the captain rarely noticed that the sailor was dead until he'd already left the harbor. In fact, some crimps sold a captain a corpse or a dummy on purpose. Herbert Asbury observes, "Many murder mysteries in early San Francisco were never solved because of this practice of shipping the *corpus delicti* to sea as a live sailor; many crimps did a flourishing business in so disposing of the victims of criminals."

Shanghai Kelly's Infamous Birthday Party

In the early 1870s, Shanghai Kelly staged the masterpiece of his crimping career. Three ships had docked in the harbor, but most of their crew had died or deserted. They needed almost a hundred new sailors to leave the port. One of these vessels, the *Reefer*, was notorious for its cruel captain, filthy bunks, and rancid food.

Kelly didn't see how he could find a hundred sailors, but the commission was too big to pass up. Finally he had an idea. He rented a ship called the *Goliath* for two days and announced that he was throwing a party for his birthday on board. His runners poked their heads into every bar on the waterfront and urged people to come—saying that Kelly would provide free food, drink, and entertainment as a way of saying "thank you" to all the other crimps and runners who had helped him all these years. Almost everyone on the waterfront headed for the *Goliath* and found Kelly's bartenders on board, serving free whiskey and food. When the party got going, Kelly pulled up the gangplank and headed for the Golden Gate, where the *Reefer* and its companion ships were waiting. By this time, the bartenders had laced the drinks with opium, and the guests were stumbling and passing out on the deck. When all the revelers had finally collapsed, Kelly and his runners hauled their comatose bodies off the *Goliath* and divided them among the three ships. The grateful captains paid Kelly several thousand dollars.

As the *Goliath* sailed back toward San Francisco, Kelly realized that everyone on the waterfront knew about his birthday party and had watched him leave port with a ship full of guests. But only Kelly and his bartenders and runners were returning. How would he explain that? As he waited for nightfall, he had a stroke of luck. The *Goliath* got word that a ship named the *Yankee Blade* had hit a rock and was sinking. Kelly steered the *Goliath* toward the distressed ship and saved everyone on board. Since the previous guests had passed out before they could finish the drink and food, the bartenders began mixing drinks for the new passengers, and Kelly announced that it was his birthday. When the *Goliath* finally reached the Montgomery Street pier, the drunken crew of the *Yankee Blade* stumbled off and wandered into the waterfront bars. Anyone who asked about Kelly's birthday party got an incoherent answer that the party was great.

San Francisco is a city where people are never more abroad than when they are at home.

— Benjamin F. Taylor

Black Bart, the Gentleman Robber

Black Bart was always a gentleman when he robbed Wells Fargo stagecoaches. He dressed in black and wore a flour sack over his head with eyeholes cut out. Jumping in front of the horses, Bart would brandish a double-barreled shotgun and command the stagecoach driver to stop and "throw down the box" that contained cash, checks, and sometimes jewelry. The driver invariably described the robber as soft-spoken and courteous. Following Bart's first stagecoach robbery in the summer of 1877, Wells Fargo officers searched the scene of the crime and found the empty metal box with a poem inside:

I've labored long and hard for bread
For honor and for riches
But on my corns too long you've trod,
You fine-haired sons of bitches.
—Black Bart

On July 25, 1878, Bart robbed his second Wells Fargo stagecoach. This time the driver noticed his blue eyes peering through the holes of the flour sack. He also realized that the robber was wearing a derby hat under his hood. Once again, Bart made off with the contents of the strongbox and left a poem in exchange:

Here I lay me down to sleep
To wait the coming morrow.
Perhaps success, perhaps defeat,
And everlasting sorrow.
Let come what will—I'll try it on,
My condition can't be worse.
And if there's money in that box,
'Tis money in my purse.
—Black Bart, the PO8

Over the next six years, Bart held up 28 Wells Fargo stagecoaches on the outskirts of Sacramento. He never raised his voice or threatened to harm a driver or passenger. During one robbery, a woman gave over her purse. Black Bart bowed and graciously returned it. "Madam, I am interested only in the Wells Fargo box and the United States mail," he said.

As the years passed, Wells Fargo kept upping the reward for Black Bart and Bart kept robbing stages and leaving poems:

So blame me not for what I've done,
I don't deserve your curses,
And if for any cause I'm hung,
Let it be for my verses!

During Bart's 28th holdup, the driver fired a rifle. The robber dropped his hat and handkerchief as he made his getaway. The authorities called in Harry N. Morse, one of the best detectives on the West Coast. Morse found a laundry mark, FOX7, on the handkerchief. Since laundries only used such marks if they had lots of customers, Morse surmised that Black Bart must live in a city. The detective went to Sacramento first, because the robberies had happened near there. He visited every laundry that used marks and sorted through the marks assigned to each customer. When he didn't find FOX7 in Sacramento, he turned to San Francisco.

San Francisco had 91 laundries. The task was exhausting, but near the end of the first week, Morse found FOX7. He asked the owner for the customer's name. It was Charles E. Bolton, a mining expert, investor, and upstanding citizen. When Morse laid eyes on the dapper 50-year-old gentleman with a large diamond ring, a weighty gold watch chain, and a diamond pin on his cravat, he knew he had his man. Charles E. Boles (Bolton's real name) served seven years for larceny.

Roving Arsonist Thugs

With lots of gold and little government, San Francisco in the 1850s attracted criminals, ex-convicts, and ticket-of-leave men from the British penal settlements at Sydney in New South Wales, Australia, and on Van Diemen's Land (later called Tasmania). These bad guys, known as Sydney Ducks or Sydney Coves, settled on the waterfront at Broadway and Pacific. The area was called Sydney-Town and later, in the mid 1860s, became known as the Barbary Coast.

The Sydney Ducks set fire to San Francisco six times between December 24, 1849 and June 22, 1851, just so they could loot the city. Each time they picked a night with southwesterly winds, so the fire would spread away from the vice district and leave Sydney-Town untouched.

Some of the dives in Sydney-Town included the Boar's Head, the Fierce Grizzly (known for unspeakable acts involving a bear), and the Goat and Compass, the favorite haunt of Dirty Tom McAlear, who would eat or drink anything for a few cents. In 1852, when Dirty Tom was arrested for "making a beast of himself," he claimed he had been drunk for seven years and could not recall the last time he had bathed. He believed it was 15 years before in England.

First Anti-Smoking Laws

In the first years of the gold rush, the "first alcalde," or mayor, was the only official who had the power to try court cases. Most of the early alcaldes didn't know much about law. One alcalde named Meade convicted all Mexicans and cigarette smokers who blew smoke out of their noses. His brand of justice anticipated the current laws against smoking in San Francisco bars and restaurants, which some people consider equally bizarre.

Best Gold Rush Lawyer

Ben Moors, the most successful lawyer in gold rush San Francisco, knew nothing about law, but had memorized the speeches of famous lawyers including Daniel Webster and John Randolph. Whatever case Moors tried, he delivered one of these speeches and usually won.

The Hounds

The Hounds, a band of 50 or 60 thugs, had once served as the muscle behind New York's corrupt Tammany Hall politicians. The U.S. Army had recruited them to fight against Mexico, and they arrived in San Francisco after the war ended. Though their regiment disbanded, the Hounds still patrolled the San Francisco streets in military uniforms, waving flags and playing fife and drum. They considered it their duty to persecute Chileans, Mexicans, and other Latin Americans.

In the summer of 1849, the Hounds dubbed themselves the Regulators and expected the citizens of San Francisco to pay them for their services. They extorted their wages by attacking merchants and robbing stores.

On July 15, 1849, the Hounds launched their most vicious raid on the Chilean settlement. Community leader Samuel Brannan persuaded the alcalde (or mayor), Doctor T. M. Leavenworth, to call for an assembly in Portsmouth Square. Brannan collected money for the Chileans who had lost their homes. Two hundred and thirty volunteers took up arms, chased down the Hounds, and jailed them on an abandoned ship. Two days later, the city held a trial. Two Hounds were sentenced to 10 years of hard labor. Others received lighter sentences, and all the Hounds had to pay fines. Within a few days, corrupt politicians had sprung the inmates from jail, but the Hounds still fled from San Francisco.

> The Hounds extorted their wages by attacking merchants and robbing stores.

Anti-Vice Crusades

Known as a city of vice, San Francisco also has a reputation for anti-vice crusades. Twice, in 1851 and 1856, citizens took the law into their own hands and established Vigilance Committees, claiming that local law enforcement was chaotic, corrupt, and in cahoots with the criminals. Everyone was apparently too busy prospecting for gold to bother with law and order.

Though the Vigilance Committees ended with the 1850s, waves of anti-vice campaigns shook the city in the 1870s, 1910s, and 1950s. By producing a glut of anti-vice propaganda, these purges also inadvertently advertised San Francisco as a den of sex and lawlessness. As a result, people seeking such decadent lifestyles flocked to the city in droves.

The Dash Club

San Francisco's anti-vice campaigns ironically promoted red-light districts such as the Barbary Coast, and later North Beach and the Tenderloin. Some crusades even made particular clubs famous. One campaign targeted Dash, a Barbary Coast dive that opened in 1908 at 574 Pacific Street and featured female impersonators. While the police condoned Dash and other naughty entertainments that brought tourist dollars to the city, anti-vice crusaders delighted in connecting the dots between local politicians and Barbary Coast dives. Dash's owner worked as a clerk for Judge Carroll Cook, who belonged to the city's corrupt political machine. Cook's opponents used Dash as a weapon against his reelection. Their campaign damaged Cook's reputation but it also propelled Dash to stardom.

The Vigilance Committee

The first Vigilance Committee formed after two men whacked merchant J. C. Jansen over the head on February 19, 1851, and robbed his store on Montgomery Street. The police apprehended Thomas Berdue, an itinerant gambler. They mistook him for a Sydney Duck named James Stuart, or English Jim. Strangely, the two men looked almost exactly alike: Each had small scar over his left eye, a slit in his left ear, and a left forefinger missing its first joint. The Sydney Ducks, like the police, believed Thomas Berdue was English Jim and plotted to avenge him.

On May 4, 1851, shortly before midnight, a fire broke out. As usual, Sydney-Town survived, as the revengeful arsonists had started the fire on a night when the winds blew away from their quarter of the city. In early June 1851, at Samuel Brannan's prompting, 200 citizens decided to take the law into their own hands, resulting in the creation of the original Vigilance Committee.

English Jim Reappears

In early July, as Thomas Berdue, who had been mistaken for English Jim, awaited execution, the real English Jim appeared in San Francisco.

The Vigilance Committee, now numbering 400 members, held the trial of English Jim on July 11, 1851. They hung Jim and exonerated Berdue.

On August 21, 1851, Governor John MacDougal denounced "the despotic control of a self-constituted association, unknown and acting in defiance of the laws." Shortly before dawn Sheriff Jack Hayes showed up at the Vigilance Committee headquarters with the police and a writ of *habeas corpus*, signed by the governor. The writ called on the vigilantes to surrender their prisoners. The vigilantes allowed the cops to escort their captives to the town jail.

On August 24, 36 vigilantes broke into the jail, seized the inmates, and swiftly took them out to be hung. The Vigilance Committee finally disbanded after hanging just three men. During these executions, each vigilante took a turn holding the rope. This deterred the city from prosecuting the vigilantes. All the members of the Vigilance Committee had participated in the executions, and the city did not want to spend the time or money prosecuting hundreds of men.

David Terry, Supreme Court Thug

David Terry was a zealous proponent of wrong causes. A member of the white supremacist Know-Nothing Party, he supported slavery in California. He also served as a justice on the California Supreme Court from 1856 to 1859, when the Know-Nothings disguised themselves as the "American Party" and swept the elections.

As a Supreme Court justice, Terry carried a bowie knife in his belt and did not hesitate to use it. When San Francisco's second Vigilance Committee formed in 1856, Terry considered it a personal affront to an elected official like himself. He sent the vigilantes an order to surrender their prisoners to state authorities. When the vigilantes ignored the order, Terry charged into the Vigilance Committee headquarters and stabbed the deputy in the neck with his bowie knife. The horrified Vigilance Committee took Terry into custody, as he whined about being arrested "merely for sticking a knife into a damn little Yankee well-borer." When the people of San Francisco heard that the deputy's life was in danger, an angry mob surrounded the jail, howling, "Hang Terry! Hang Terry!"

The vigilantes tried Terry and found him guilty, but they were reluctant to hang a Supreme Court justice. They eventually discharged him at night and rushed him out of San Francisco so he wouldn't be mauled by the mob.

At the start of the Civil War, Terry continued his pursuit of doomed causes by pressuring California to secede from the Union. When that failed, he went to fight for the South at Chickamauga. Seeing that the Confederate army was losing, Terry journeyed to Texas and assembled his own military. But before he could attack the Union army, Robert E. Lee surrendered. Terry didn't want to disband a good army without conquering someone, so he marched his troops across the border to Mexico and tried to overthrow Maximilian, the Mexican emperor. Failing to conquer Mexico, he finally returned to San Francisco, scorned as a murderer and traitor.

At 61, David Terry found his swan song of lost causes. In 1884, Sarah Althea Hill retained him as her attorney in one of the strangest and most sensational divorce cases in San Francisco history. Hill charged Senator William Sharon with adultery and sued for a divorce. When Sharon swore he'd never married Hill, she produced a tattered wedding certificate. She testified that Sharon hadn't wanted to marry her. He had simply offered her a monthly stipend for sleeping with him, but she'd insisted on marriage and had the wedding certificate to prove it.

She said the document was tattered because Sharon had asked for it back and when she refused, he then tried to rip it out of her hands and strangle her. Sharon claimed the contract was counterfeit, but the state court believed Hill's testimony and granted her a divorce. She was awarded $2,500 a month in alimony.

Sharon was so shocked he died of apoplexy. Terry promptly married Hill, the heir to Sharon's estate. But before the senator died, he had appealed to a higher court and directed the executors of his will to use whatever funds necessary to overturn the verdict, so his rightful heirs would inherit his estate instead of Hill.

One month after Sharon's death, the California Supreme Court ruled that Hill's marriage contract was a forgery.

When Judge Stephen J. Field read the verdict, Hill stood up and shouted that Sharon's family had bribed him. She refused to sit down and clawed at the bailiffs as they removed her from the courtroom. Terry drew his bowie knife and yelled, "You sons of bitches! I'll cut you to pieces!" The guards seized him and dragged him out of the court too. Hill didn't stop fighting until the guards eventually tied her up. They discovered a loaded gun in her purse. When the bailiffs had finally subdued both Terrys and locked them in jail, Judge Field finished reading the verdict.

Terry and Hill served six months in prison for contempt of court. They spent their time stewing and plotting revenge. As their sentence came to an end, Judge Field hired a bodyguard to protect him from them.

On August 14, 1889, several weeks after the couple's release, the judge was traveling on Southern Pacific's red-eye train from Los Angeles to San Francisco. When the train stopped in Fresno at 3:00 A.M., Field's bodyguard, U.S. Marshal David Neagle, spotted Terry and Hill boarding the train. He advised the infirm, 73-year-old Field to stay in his compartment when the train stopped in Lathrop for breakfast.

Field didn't listen. He got off at Lathrop and shuffled into the station's dining room for breakfast. Neagle stood near his charge. When Terry entered the dining room, he cocked his gun. He walked up behind Field and slapped the judge on the side of his head, then on the back. Neagle whipped out his gun and fired two shots. Terry crumpled to the floor. The other passengers in the dining hall screamed. When Hill saw Terry in a pool of blood, she drew her gun, but the dining-hall manager stopped her before she could fire. Judge Field quietly stood up, wiped his mustache with his napkin, and walked back to the train.

After Terry died, his paramour Hill became obsessed with spiritualism, which was popular at the time. She sought out mediums to communicate with her dead husband.

Mary Ellen Pleasant, a powerful African-American entrepreneur, looked after Hill. But by 1892, she found Hill's behavior so disturbing that Pleasant sought to have her committed to a mental institution. Judge Walter H. Levy, who had been one of the lawyers representing Hill in her case against Sharon, sent Hill to the Stockton State Hospital for the Insane, where she spent the remaining 45 years of her life.

If civil disobedience is the way to go about change, then I think a lot of people will be going to San Francisco.

— Rosie O'Donnell

The Busy Mercenary

William Walker, an ambitious soldier of fortune, first came to San Francisco in 1850 at the age of 26. After several years as a journalist, he decided to pursue a more adventurous career waging unauthorized wars against Latin American countries, even though the U.S. was at peace with these nations.

In 1853, Walker invaded Baja, Mexico and declared it an independent republic. He then tried to annex Sonora, which also belonged to Mexico. When his invasion failed, he came back to San Francisco and was tried for violating U.S. neutrality laws. Walker was acquitted, and in June 1855, he set off on his next mission: an invasion of Nicaragua.

> Walker was acquitted, and in June 1855, he set off on his next mission: an invasion of Nicaragua.

Nicaraguan Liberals, who were at war with the Conservative Party, welcomed Walker at first. But Walker had his own plans for Latin America. He wanted to institute a system of slavery like that in the American South. In 1856, Walker seized and destroyed the beautiful city of Granada, proclaiming himself president of Nicaragua. Neighboring Central American countries raised an army and quickly overthrew him. Walker was again tried for violating neutrality and again acquitted. Many of his contemporaries viewed him as a hero, even though from today's perspective he looks like a racist megalomaniac. In 1860, Walker made his last attempt to conquer Latin America. The British navy arrested him in Honduras and turned him over to local authorities, who executed him by firing squad.

Men Fight over Courtesan

On November 15, 1855, the Italian gambler Charles Cora took his mistress Belle Cora (aka Arabella Ryan) to see a production at the American Theatre in San Francisco. Madame Cora ran a brothel on Pike Street, now Waverly Place, where the most beautiful and expensive women worked. General W. H. Richardson, United States Marshal for the Northern District of California, was also at the show that evening. He demanded that the theater kick out Belle Cora. When the theater refused to remove her, Richardson argued with Charles Cora. The Italian shot and killed General Richardson several days later.

James King, editor of the *Evening Bulletin*—an anti-vice paper seeking to rid the city of gambling and prostitution—published editorials calling for the death penalty and predicting that Charles Cora's corrupt political allies would see that he was acquitted. King's attack on Cora led to crossfire of vicious editorials with James P. Casey, who edited a political paper and served on the Board of Supervisors. The accusations escalated for several months. On May 14, editor Casey appeared at the door of the *Bulletin* and shot editor King in the chest as he left work. A few days later King died.

That night an angry mob gathered around the jail. The citizens had formed the second Vigilance Committee by the next day. At noon, the chair of the committee, William T. Coleman, surrounded the jail with 2,600 armed men and demanded the surrender of Cora and Casey. The vigilantes manacled the two prisoners and took them to the committee's headquarters. The mob followed, demanding that Charles Cora and editor Casey be hanged at once. The vigilantes hanged the two men from the windows of their headquarters. Cora married Belle an hour before he went to the gallows.

On June 3, 1856, the governor declared that San Francisco was in a state of insurrection. He commanded the vigilantes to lay down their arms and disband. They surrendered on August 18.

Once I knew the City very well, spent my attic days there, while others were being a lost generation in Paris, I fledged in San Francisco, climbed its hills, slept in its parks, worked on its docks, marched and shouted in its revolts . . . It had been to me in the days of my poverty and it did not resent my temporary solvency.

– John Steinbeck

The Barbary Coast

San Francisco's "Barbary Coast" got its name in the mid 1860s from the Barbary Coast of North Africa, where marauding pirates preyed on ships. By the 1870s, local authorities had confined the brothels, dives, and dance halls to a 35-block district bounded by Stockton, Kearny, Broadway, and Market Streets. The Barbary Coast reigned as the nation's most notorious red-light district until 1917. In the most highly concentrated areas, virtually every building served as a brothel or bar where "pretty waiter girls" sold drinks and other services. From the 1860s to the 1880s, local newspapers referred to the thieves and saloon keepers of the area as Rangers. On November 28, 1869, the *San Francisco Call* reported:

> *The Barbary Coast! That mysterious region so much talked of; so seldom visited! Of which so much is heard, but little seen! … The coast on which no gentle breezes blow, but where rages one wild sirocco of sin! … Night is the time to visit the Coast. In the daytime it is dull and unattractive, seeming but a cesspool of rottenness, the air is impregnated with smells more pungent than polite; but when night lets fall its dusky curtain, the Coast brightens into life, and becomes the wild carnival of crime that has lain in lethargy during the sunny hours of the day, and now bursts forth with energy renewed by its siesta.*

The heart of the Barbary Coast was Pacific Street, which had been San Francisco's main thoroughfare at the start of the gold rush. In later years, the

Barbary Coast was synonymous with Terrific Street—a single block of Pacific between Montgomery and Kearny.

A Wild Sirocco of Sin

Three classes of brothels flourished on the Barbary Coast: the crib, cow yard, and parlor house. Each establishment was marked by a red light above its door at night and a red shade in the window during the day. Many of the small cribs contained closets with secret back doors, allowing thieves to pick money out of the customer's pockets while the crib's occupant distracted him.

Morton Street (now Maiden Lane) was a "crib alley" just off Union Square. Upright ladies passing by were greeted with catcalls, "Look out girls, here's some charity competition! Get some sense and stop giving it away!" After the 1906 fire destroyed the cribs on Morton, the street was renamed Maiden Lane in hopes of discouraging prostitution. Maiden Lane is now one of the most expensive pieces of property in San Francisco.

The cow yard—usually a three-story building containing hundreds of cribs—was considered a step up in class. The most famous, the Nymphia, opened in 1899 on Pacific near Stockton. Each of its three floors housed 150 cubicles for prostitutes. Elegant French parlor houses once lined the entire block of Commercial Street between Kearny and Grant. The door of the establishment displayed a brass or copper plaque bearing the address and the madam's name.

Although most of the parlor-house buildings have been torn down, one still stands at 742 Commercial—the former home of Madame Marcelle's Parisian Mansion. One customer showed up at the Parisian Mansion each morning, changed into women's clothes, swept and dusted the entire building, paid a silver dollar, then left. Madame Marcelle never revealed his name.

Devil's Acre

The 19th-century Barbary Coast was a hotbed of violent crime. In the 1880s, the pie-shaped block between Broadway, Kearny, and Columbus (then Montgomery Avenue) was called Devil's Acre. The east side of Kearny, known as Battle Row, was lined with low-end "cribs" that witnessed one murder a week and five brawls a day.

Outlawing the Cancan

In the 1860s and 1870s, the *San Francisco Call* raised public support a law forbidding women to work in dance halls. This would have put the dance halls out of business, since these men's clubs featured women dancing the outrageous cancan. An ordinance was enacted in 1869 and again in 1876, but neither was enforced. When the *San Francisco Chronicle* got involved in 1879, the city passed a law against the cancan. In March 1879, the police arrested Mabel Santley, a cancan dancer, for indecent exposure. Though Miss Santley wore long skirts, she refused to keep them around her ankles.

Nineteenth-Century Junkies Shock Tourists

"Hoppies"—the junkies of the late 19th-century Barbary Coast—lived in the alleys of the vice district and Chinatown. They made a living by panhandling, running errands for madams and prostitutes, and gathering wood and boxes to sell. Sometimes tourists would pay them a few cents to see the holes in their arms.

Most hoppies couldn't afford a hypodermic needle, so they filled a medicine dropper with cocaine or morphine and jabbed the tip into their flesh. Cocaine and morphine were both legal at the time. The hoppies bought most of their drugs from a 24-hour drugstore on Grant Avenue, which sold one injection's worth of cocaine or morphine for 10 to 15 cents.

In response to rising hysteria about white middle- and upper-class youths frequenting Chinatown's opium dens, San Francisco passed the first anti-drug law in the U.S. in 1875. The city ordinance forbade opium smoking "under heavy fine, imprisonment, or both." The police enforced the law only against white people and not against the Chinese.

Laws Against the Chinese

In the 1870s, San Francisco passed a number of ordinances intended to harass Chinese immigrants. One law made it illegal to carry baskets from poles supported on one's shoulders. Another outlawed disinterring bodies. This law was not meant to prevent grave vandalism or the spread of disease, but to keep the Chinese immigrants from sending their dead home to China for burial. A third law required everyone who worked in a Chinese laundry to pay a tax of $15 each quarter. Since the Chinese lived in severely overcrowded conditions, the city also prohibited sleeping in a room with fewer than 500 cubic feet per person and fined offenders between $10 and $50. On June 14, 1876, the Board of Supervisors passed a statute requiring the hair of every man in the jail to be cut within an inch of his scalp. This law ensured that a Chinese man who was arrested would lose his queue—the braid he wore as a Chinese custom.

Shortly after the haircut law was passed, the cops arrested Ho Ah Kow for sleeping in too small a room. When the jailor Matthew Noonan cut off Ho Ah Kow's queue, he sued Noonan and the Board of Supervisors for $10,000, alleging that his haircut damaged his reputation in the eyes of fellow Chinese immigrants. In 1879, the Circuit Court found the queue law invalid. Ho Ah Kow received a settlement of several hundred dollars.

The Hoodlums Are Born

The hoodlums were particular to San Francisco, though identical in behavior to the hooligans of London and the bullies and roughs of the Bowery and Five Points of New York. The word "hoodlum" first appeared in San Francisco newspapers in mid 1868. Though the word's origins are unknown, the most likely story is that the *San Francisco Times* published an article describing the practices of a gang of boys who shouted the password "Huddle 'em! Huddle 'em!" as a cue to surround their victim in a huddle, like a contemporary football team.

> *Most were boys and men between 12 and 30 years old. Girl hoodlums were usually fiercer than their male counterparts.*

Hoodlums were proud of their name. They traveled in packs and especially enjoyed tormenting Chinese immigrants. Most were boys and men between 12 and 30 years old. Girl hoodlums were usually fiercer than their male counterparts. Hoodlums rarely carried guns. They preferred their fists, but also fought with clubs, knives, and brass or iron knuckles that fit on their hands like gloves. In the late 1880s the typical hoodlum dressed like a dandy, but was caked in dirt. He wore a ruffled white shirt with a black string tie, a velvet vest, a frock coat, tight pants, calfskin boots, and last but not least … a sombrero.

The Barbary Coast Burns

The fire following the 1906 earthquake leveled the Barbary Coast, but it rose from the ashes almost overnight. The post-1906 Barbary Coast was tame and gentrified compared to its 19th-century incarnation. After the quake, it became a tourist mecca for middle-class youth. Every establishment charged exorbitant prices and geared their shows to shock sightseers without scaring them away. Between 1906 and 1917, brothels and dance halls lined the entire 500 block of Pacific except the firehouse at 515.

Some of these structures remain standing, including the Little Fox Theatre Building at 535 Pacific; the Thalia Building at 544–550 Pacific; the Hippodrome at 555 Pacific; and the site of Dash, a club featuring female impersonators, at 574 Pacific.

Judges Close Brothels

The Barbary Coast closed in 1917, when the California Supreme Court joined 31 other states in declaring the Red Light Abatement Act constitutional. The Temperance Movement and mounting concern about syphilis influenced this ruling. On February 14, police raided the Barbary Coast, closing 83 brothels and throwing 1,073 women out on the streets. Thousands of dressmakers, laundresses, housemaids, brothel musicians, and others who made a living indirectly from prostitution, also lost their jobs. Prostitution was so central to the neighborhood that when the brothels shut down, the entire Barbary Coast economy collapsed.

"The Wettest of the West"

During Prohibition, from 1920 to 1933, San Francisco openly defied both federal and state bans against alcohol. The city—dubbed the "wettest of the west"—remained thoroughly committed to drinking, producing, and distributing liquor.

At the 1920 Democratic National Convention in San Francisco, municipal leaders scored a carload of the finest bourbon whiskey, which dazzled delegates accustomed to "paint remover and sheep dip." Elegant ladies greeted delegates at their hotels with free quart bottles, compliments of Mayor "Sunny Jim" Rolph.

In 1926, the Board of Supervisors even passed a resolution opposing police enforcement of prohibition. They sent copies of the resolution to the San Francisco police chief, the state senate, and the federal administrators of Prohibition.

The Tenderloin District

San Francisco's Tenderloin district lies downtown between Market Street, Van Ness Avenue, and Union Square. In the late 19th century, the cops who patrolled this crime-ridden area received higher salaries and thus bought better cuts of meat—hence the name "Tenderloin." Today, the Tenderloin abuts fancy downtown hotels, but still attracts the down and out. It has one of the highest crimes rates in San Francisco, despite the policing.

Cops Impersonate Gay Men

In the 1950s—the era of McCarthyism and the cold war—undercover agents posed as gay men. They hung out in gay bars flirting with patrons in an effort to entrap them. Under extremely broad interpretations of the law, people were arrested for same-sex kissing, touching, and dancing. Beginning in 1955, cross-gender behavior and dress were also construed as illegal. Women dressed in men's clothes would wear women's panties, believing that if they wore one article of women's clothing, the police couldn't arrest them for impersonating men. Drag queens wore men's underwear for the same reason.

Patty Hearst Joins the Symbionese Liberation Army

In 1974, William Randolph Hearst's 19-year-old granddaughter Patty walked into Hibernia Bank, at 1450 Noriega and 22nd Avenue, wielding a semiautomatic weapon. Two months earlier, Hearst had been kidnapped from her apartment at 2603 Benvenue Avenue in Berkeley. The media had portrayed her as a victim. But when the bank's surveillance cameras caught her with a gun, she became

America's most wanted terrorist overnight. Why would a multimillionaire heiress need to rob a bank? It seemed she had sided with her captors.

In 1975, Hearst was arrested with her Symbionese Liberation Army kidnappers at 625 Morse Street in San Francisco. Her defense attorney, F. Lee Bailey, argued that she had been brainwashed. Though Hearst wore a T-shirt that said "Pardon Me" to court, she received seven years for armed robbery. She served a total of 30 months before President Carter granted her clemency.

Hearst later married her bodyguard, Bernard Shaw. Bizarrely, her maid of honor was Trish Robbin—whose father owned the same Hibernia Bank that Hearst had robbed.

I will sing in San Francisco if I have to sing in the streets, for I know that the streets of San Francisco are free.

— Luisa Tetrazzini, soprano

A Flasher Called God

On February 14, 1996, a man calling himself Mr. Ubiquitous Perpetuity God began serving a nine-month sentence in the Marin County Jail for indecent exposure. Born Enrique Silberg, Mr. God immigrated to the U.S. from Cuba. He legally changed his name in 1985 so his victims would have "some type of awareness of

God." Court-appointed psychiatrist Dr. Diane McEwen of Tiburon said Mr. God, 68, suffers from "a severe psychotic delusional disorder." At the hearing, Marin Superior Court Judge Lynn O'Malley Taylor said Mr. God "will be released to a residential mental health facility if one agrees to admit him."

The Parrot Testifies

In November 1994, a San Francisco defense attorney summoned a parrot to the witness stand to testify about the murder of its owner. The judge refused to hear the bird's testimony, even though animals had taken the stand in two other national court cases earlier that year.

In the spring of 1994, a chicken had appeared as a witness in Tyler, Texas to help demonstrate a prison vaccination protocol. That same spring, a defense attorney called a police dog to the stand in Pittsburgh, Pennsylvania to demonstrate that the dog, rather than his client, had started a fight. History does not record how he proved that the dog was the bully.

The Dummy Police Officer

San Francisco police officer Bob Geary worked his North Beach beat with his ventriloquist's dummy Brendan O'Smarty. One day, the chief said O'Smarty had to go. Geary gathered signatures and submitted a proposition to the ballot. In the 1993 election, the majority of San Francisco voters said yes, the puppet should remain on patrol. But the IRS was unconvinced when Geary attempted to deduct his election expenses on his tax return.

Paid for Potty Trauma

In May 1991, a construction worker in the San Francisco Bay Area sued for damages after a forklift picked up the portable toilet he was using and carried it to another location. The plaintiff won $89,000. News sources did not mention whether his injuries were physical or psychological.

Thief Knifes Self

Wayne Manns was hospitalized in April 1992 as a result of injuries sustained while shoplifting at San Francisco's Emporium department store. Security guards said Manns tucked six kitchen knives into the waistband of his pants and tried to slip out the exit door. As the guards apprehended him, he stabbed himself.

The CIA Acid Tests: Dosing Unsuspecting Citizens with LSD

The CIA brought LSD to San Francisco for research purposes more than a decade before the counterculture championed the drug. During the cold war, intelligence agencies searched for a truth serum that would prompt an enemy spy to reveal military secrets during interrogation. Convinced that the Soviets were developing psychoactive drugs as intelligence weapons, the CIA launched the top-secret Operation MK-ULTRA in 1953 to test the uses of such drugs for mind control and espionage.

In secret experiments on soldiers and government personnel, LSD proved too unpredictable to use in interrogation. People under its influence did not always provide accurate information. Those who took the drug often experienced extreme distortions of space, time, and body image, sometimes triggering anxiety attacks and full-blown paranoia. CIA researchers concluded that LSD could actually hinder an interrogation as the enemy spy might realize he'd been drugged, become acutely suspicious, and refuse to reveal any information.

The colorless, odorless drug was easy to hide in food or drinks, and even micrograms produced dramatic effects.

Though LSD didn't work as a truth serum, it was simply too interesting for the agency to set aside. The colorless, odorless, tasteless drug was easy to hide in food or drinks, and even micrograms produced dramatic effects. Researchers looked for other ways to use it. They considered dosing leaders of left-wing governments to make them act strangely in public or while giving a speech. Agents also dosed each other to see what would happen if someone took LSD under everyday circumstances. On numerous occasions, pranking agents spiked each other's drinks at social gatherings. In 1954, several agents conspired to sprinkle the drug in the punch bowl at the annual Christmas party.

Finally, the CIA decided to test LSD on unsuspecting American citizens in real-life situations. The agency conducted many of its experiments in San Francisco.

CIA Odd Jobs

George Hunter White had an odd job. A narcotics officer by day, he busted drug sellers on the streets of San Francisco; by night, he ran a CIA brothel that spiked men's drinks with LSD. During his off hours, he threw rowdy parties for his buddies in the safe house. Neighbors complained about men with shoulder-harnessed guns chasing scantily clad women around the yard. White couldn't always handle his double life. A friend who stopped by the safe house once found him downing a bottle of Gibson's gin and shooting wax slugs at his own reflection in the mirror.

There is no definitive record of when the CIA stopped testing LSD, but White seems to have parted ways with the CIA when he retired in 1966. In a letter to Dr. Sidney Gottlieb, who ran the MK-ULTRA program, White described his work in San Francisco:

I was a very minor missionary, actually a heretic, but I toiled wholeheartedly in the vineyard because it was fun, fun, fun. Where else could a red-blooded American boy lie, kill, cheat, steal, rape, and pillage with the blessing of the All-Highest?

By the time White retired, the CIA had a "stable of drugs," including acid (code named P-1), for use in covert operations. It was thought to be Army scientists who coined the word "trip" for an LSD session.

The Medical Marijuana Movement

Since the passage of the Compassionate Use Act (Proposition 215), California's 1996 medical marijuana law, the Bay Area has become the center of a movement to allow sick people the right to use marijuana. In the Bay Area, more than 45 medical cannabis dispensaries sell high-quality cannabis and locally produced hashish, plus marijuana candies, baked goods, and tinctures for those too ill to smoke. Both outside and within controlled indoor grow rooms, marijuana growing is big business in the San Francisco area. State law permits patients to grow their own medical cannabis or to select a caregiver to grow it for them. The amount one is allowed to grow varies from town to town. The plant remains the largest cash crop in California, the nation's number one agricultural state.

Virgin Marries Death Row Inmate

On October 3, 1996, self-proclaimed virgin Doreen Lioy, 41 of San Rafael married death-row inmate Richard Ramirez, 36, in the visiting room of San Quentin. Ramirez, also known as the "Night Stalker," terrorized Los Angeles and the San Francisco Bay Area in 1985. Lioy grew up Roman Catholic, but she accommodated her spouse's Satanism. Though she purchased a gold wedding band for herself, she bought a platinum one for her fiancé, because Ramirez said Satanists don't wear gold. They won't be able to consummate their marriage, because death row inmates aren't allowed conjugal visits.

Since Ramirez's arrest in 1985, Lioy has written him at least 75 letters. He proposed in 1988, but due to prison regulations, they had to wait until 1996 to wed. Meanwhile, slews of other suitors competed for his attentions. Lioy reportedly ran into other women during visiting hours, and more than one threatened to beat her up if she didn't back off. But Lioy held her ground. What could the attraction be? Ramirez currently remains on death row awaiting execution.

Mystery of the Zodiac Killer

One of the strangest cases in San Francisco's criminal history was a spate of serial murders known as the Zodiac killings. The police linked the Zodiac to five homicides and two assaults between December 1968 and October 1969, but the

Zodiac's reign of terror lasted much longer in the sense that San Francisco residents lived in fear of the killer for at least five years. While the killer captured the national imagination, he also became obsessed with his own image in the media. Between 1969 and 1974, the killer sent the police and newspapers taunting letters—boasting of his achievements and threatening more deaths unless they published his missives. These letters were so gruesomely detailed that they could only have come from the slayer himself. Each letter opened with the phrase, "This is the Zodiac speaking."

The first, apparently motiveless, killing occurred in 1968 when two high school students were shot as they fled from their car. The next murder was in July 1969, and shortly after, the police received a mysterious phone call bragging about the murder.

A month later, three newspapers received coded messages from the murderer. The Zodiac killer continued his murderous spree over the next few months, keeping in contact at all times with San Francisco newspapers. In October, he sent a shred of bloodstained shirt to the *San Francisco Chronicle,* with a letter complaining about police incompetence.

The Zodiac killer continued to correspond with police until 1974. Then nothing more was heard. The murders also ceased, leaving San Francisco police with an open file that remains unsolved to this day.

PART III:
Urban Myths

One day if I do go to heaven... I'll look around and say, "It ain't bad, but it ain't San Francisco."

– Herb Caen

I love this city. If I'm elected, I will move the White House to San Francisco.

– Robert Kennedy

There are some stories that remain ingrained in California's collective consciousness—regardless of whether or not they are actually based on facts. With San Francisco's outlandish history, it is no surprise that the city has given birth to some incredibly tall tales. For example, in the 19th century, it was claimed that a labyrinth of underground tunnels riddled Chinatown. Today, most historians don't think the tunnels ever existed, but some insist they did. Others claim the Chinese had connected six or seven neighboring cellars, which word of mouth exaggerated into a maze of underground passageways.

Another myth still circulating is that James Marshall discovered gold in California in January 1848, when in fact it was discovered in 1846. Like other urban legends, the story of James Marshall spread by hearsay and changed over time. No one knows who created the myth, but we know why it started. The government wanted to wait until it officially had control of California before announcing the discovery of gold. Another false rumor is the widespread belief that Mark Twain coined the phrase, "The coldest winter I ever spent was a summer in San Francisco."

Just for kicks we've also thrown in some theories that have neither been proven true nor false, so the reality remains an eternal mystery. British submarine commander Gavin Menzies offered compelling evidence that the Chinese had shipwrecked near San Francisco in 1421. Many professional historians question Menzies's research methods, but now the story has taken on a life of its own.

How about that car that fell through the gap in the Bay Bridge during the 1989 Loma Prieta earthquake? Millions of people watched on television as the car plunged into the bay, starting many rumors about who the passengers actually were. Were they truly lovers who feared their affair would be discovered if they stopped?

This chapter contains the most amusing and outrageous urban myths, from cases of innocent Chinese whispers to deliberate political smoke screens.

Who Discovered Gold in California?

Many history books claim that James W. Marshall discovered the gold that launched the gold rush in January 1848. Marshall was building a sawmill for John Augustus Sutter in the Sierra Nevada foothills. In order to power the mill, he dug a channel that filled with water from the American River. The rushing water rinsed away loose pebbles, revealing particles of gold.

There are numerous stories about what happened next. Some say Sutter swore Marshall to secrecy, but a servant overheard them. Others say Sutter convinced Marshall it was pyrite. For the next several weeks, they threw the sparkling pebbles away—until a nugget got into the hands of Isaac Humphrey, who recognized it as gold and started prospecting. Others say Samuel Brannan filled a sack with gold dust and rode to San Francisco shouting, "There's gold in them thar hills."

Once the word got out, fortune seekers overran Sutter's land, tore down his buildings, killed his cattle, and ruined his crops as they picked gold off the leaves and roots. Sutter lost everything. He spent the last years of his life petitioning

Congress for reparations. Congress refused. Marshall fared no better than Sutter. He sold his share of the mill for $2,000 and never found any more gold. The miners suspected he was withholding information about richer deposits of gold and threatened to lynch him if he didn't tell. Marshall fled and died a drunkard.

Traditional U.S. history places Marshall's discovery of gold on the date of January 24, 1848—nine days before the Treaty of Guadalupe Hidalgo gave almost half of Mexico to the United States. In *Imperial San Francisco*, historian Gray Brechin presents evidence that "Marshall merely rediscovered gold. High officials in Washington, D.C. knew that California possessed gold and much else besides, before declaring war on its neighbor." Thomas O. Larkin, U.S. consul to Mexico, sent word of California's mineral riches to Captain John Montgomery and President James Buchanan on May 2 and 4, 1846. On May 11, 1846, the United States declared war on Mexico, presumably due to a border dispute. Perhaps San Francisco's motto, "Gold in Peace, Iron in War," should be changed to simply "Gold in War."

President James Knox Polk officially launched the gold rush on December 5, 1848, when he showed Congress a 14-pound nugget of California gold. By that time, Washington had known about the gold for at least two and a half years.

Where the Miners Came From

The idea that "miner forty-niners" were predominantly Americans from the East Coast who went west for the gold rush is a very old urban myth. Between 1850 and 1860, more than 50 percent of the people living in San Francisco were foreign-born, compared to 10 percent in other U.S. cities. The first miners came from Valparaiso, Chile, and Lima, Peru, Latin American port cities with long histories of gold mining and trading with San Francisco. Many also came from the Guangdong province in southern China. By 1876, more than 100,000 Chinese had immigrated to California. Most of them settled in San Francisco—forming the largest Chinatown in the U.S. Many of these immigrants labored on the Union Pacific Railroad.

Medieval Chinese Junk Shipwrecks Near San Francisco Bay

The Chinese may have explored northern California before the Spanish arrived. The wreck of a medieval Chinese junk lies under a sandbank in the Sacramento River, northeast of the San Francisco Bay. Dr. John Furry of the Natural History Museum of Northern California first learned of the junk 20 years ago. Carbon dating showed that the vessel was built in 1410.

The junk, along with other compelling evidence, led amateur historian Gavin Menzies to claim that the Chinese landed near San Francisco in 1421. Menzies speculates that some Chinese voyagers stayed in the Bay Area and blended in with the native California Indians, who settled there thousands of years earlier.

Opera Singer Flees Quake

Opera singer Enrico Caruso was staying at the Sheraton Palace Hotel, 650 Market Street, when the 1906 earthquake struck. He supposedly dashed out of the hotel with only a towel wrapped around his waist and swore he'd never return to the city. Caruso, who prided himself on his macho bearing, later disputed this account and specifically refuted reports that he had left the hotel crying.

A President Poisoned by His Wife?

President Warren G. Harding died in San Francisco—perhaps after being poisoned by his wife. Harding had recently had an affair with a woman named Nan Britton. When Britton moved to D.C. and began having trysts with Harding at the White House, Mrs. Harding grilled government agent Gaston Means for information about a deadly white powder. The president and his entourage were returning from an Alaskan vacation when Harding fell sick with what looked like food poisoning in Vancouver. They continued on the train to San Francisco. On July 29, 1923, Harding checked into the Presidential Suite of the Palace Hotel, then checked out for good. He died there on August 2.

Mayor Starts Fires after 1906 Earthquake

Shortly after Mayor Eugene Schmitz had been indicted for graft, the 1906 earthquake hit. Fire broke out and consumed the mayor's business records along with two-thirds of the city. Rumor has it that the mayor may have started some of the fires himself. Some say a local farmer offered to flood San Francisco with his dredger to put out the fire, but Mayor Schmitz said no thanks. After the quake, the city heralded Schmitz as a hero for his response to the disaster.

The Matchmaking Busybody

Mary Ellen Pleasant—whom we first encountered in Part I—was a magnet for urban myths and strange rumors. According to one story, she ensured her power over banker Thomas Bell by marrying him to Theresa Perry, a girl whom Pleasant saved from poverty. Pleasant built an opulent 30-room mansion at 1661 Octavia that she would live in with Bell and Theresa (neither of whom had a clue about her plans). Secret passageways between rooms would permit Pleasant to spy on the other occupants.

Theresa was already indebted to Pleasant, who had taught her aristocratic manners, encouraged her to shoot a tiresome ex-husband, and helped her conceal the murder. Legend has it that one night Pleasant drugged Bell and married him off to Theresa. Soon the three were living in the house together, as Pleasant had planned. As the years passed, Pleasant continued to control Bell by hiring newly pregnant young women to seduce him and later claim that they were carrying his child. Pleasant then arranged for the children to be delivered in secret and raised as part of the family. Bell was forever indebted to her for keeping his secrets.

Leaving San Francisco is like saying goodbye to an old sweetheart. You want to linger as long as possible.

— Walter Cronkite

Ill-Starred Lovers Perish in Earthquake

In 1989, the Loma Prieta earthquake rattled the San Francisco area, killing 69 people and injuring almost 4,000. Measuring 6.9 on the Richter scale, it cracked open the Bay Bridge that links San Francisco to Oakland, the city across the bay.

The earthquake severed the bridge, leaving a gap in the roadway. An intrepid motorcyclist jumped off his bike and flagged down cars heading for the fateful gap. But one car forged ahead. According to local

According to local legend, the car contained two immigrants from India who were having a secret love affair.

legend, the car contained two immigrants from India who were having a secret love affair and feared that they would be discovered.

Deciding to take the risk, the lovers ignored the warning and gunned their engine, trying to leap the breach in the pavement. Their car fell through the gap and plunged into the bay, never to be seen again. San Francisco residents watched in horror as TV news showed footage of the car's nosedive.

The Inflatable Bra

This myth came from the Herb Caen column in the *San Francisco Chronicle*:

> *The national sales manager for an inflatable bra—created for the girls that nature had short-changed—apparently was flying from Los Angeles to San Francisco with his most popular model. She was, of course, loyally wearing one of the boss's products. It turned out that the plane had a nonpressurized cabin, and the higher they flew the more inflated the brassiere became. It was so nerve-racking for the other passengers that she finally had to retreat to the pilot's compartment. She finished the flight there, gradually deflating.*

Legendary Outlaw

Joaquin Murieta (born Carillo) was a Chilean outlaw and the subject of the poem *The Life and Adventures of Joaquin Murieta: The Celebrated California Bandit,* published in 1854 by John Rollin Ridge (aka Yellow Bird), the grandson of a Cherokee chief. According to myth, Murieta became an outlaw after gringo miners slaughtered his family. Murieta's band included Three-Fingered Jack (born Manuel Garcia) and Murieta's wife Rosita Felix (later Antonia Molinera), who had short hair, wore men's clothing, and took part in the outlaw's killings and robberies.

In August 1853, Mexican War veteran Harry S. Love claimed to have Murieta's severed head. The head was displayed at the corner of Halleck and Sansome Streets for a fee of $1.00 per person. Though the head was never positively identified as Murieta's, it became something of a legend, especially because its hair continued to grow.

Underground Tunnels

A nineenth-century legend claims that San Francisco gangsters evaded the cops by slipping into a network of tunnels that lay beneath Chinatown. The San Francisco police believed in these tunnels, based on numerous testimonies. Witnesses claimed to have traveled through the passageways and described underground businesses and hideouts.

When the fire of 1906 razed Chinatown, the police searched for the tunnels and found nothing. Some occultists believe that the witnesses who passed through the tunnels were teleported by Chinese magicians. Most historians now consider the tunnels an urban myth. The underground passageways may have actually been a series of six or seven connected cellars, exaggerated by white San Franciscans.

In addition to the tunnels of Chinatown, it is rumored that underground passageways led from the mansions of the Nob Hill district to the brothels of the Barbary Coast. The city's elite entered the brothels through these tunnels so they didn't have to risk being seen walking in through the front doors.

Twain Endlessly Misquoted

Mark Twain, who moved to San Francisco in 1864 and took a reporting job at the *Morning Call*, has had more witticisms falsely attributed to him than most people say in their entire lifetimes. Here are some of the great quotes that Twain did not say:

The coldest winter I ever spent was a summer in San Francisco.

So I became a newspaperman. I hated to do it, but I couldn't find honest employment.

Whenever I feel the urge to exercise, I lie down until it goes away.

There are three kinds of lies: lies, damn lies, and statistics. (This was actually Benjamin Disraeli)

For every problem there is always a solution that is simple, obvious, and wrong.

The finest Congress money can buy.

The Vanishing Blimp Crew

According to the Virtual Museum of the City of San Francisco, "One of the most enduring mysteries of World War II, and one still not solved, was the disappearance of the crew of the blimp L-8 of the Navy Airship Squadron."

At 6:03 A.M. on August 16, 1942, the blimp took off from Treasure Island on a routine patrol mission. At 11:15 A.M., swimmers near the Olympic Club golf course witnessed the L-8 touch ground briefly at Ocean Beach near Fort Funston. When the airship finally crashed at 432 Bellevue Avenue in Daly City, its door was latched open, and both crew members had vanished. They were never found.

According to Dr. Eldritch Weirde, intrepid chronicler of Bay Area oddities, some ufologists and conspiracy theorists cite the blimp crew's disappearance as one of the earliest recorded UFO kidnappings. These sources claim that "a small, powerful cabal within the Pentagon has struck a deal with one or more groups of aliens, giving extraplanetary beings carte blanche to kidnap a few hundred Americans per year in exchange for technological help." The same explanation is given for southwestern sightings of cows falling from the sky "with their lips, tongues, and genitals surgically removed." Dr. Weirde writes:

> I can't figure out what the hell airmen and/or aliens want with the lips, tongues, and genitals of cattle. If they want hot dogs, it would be a lot cheaper to just buy them in a store.

Tarot Reader Curses Party Girl

In the 1960s, *Esquire Magazine* named TV show host Pat Montandon of 1000 Lombard Street one of the nation's leading party hostesses. But her "party girl" career came to an end when she threw a zodiac theme party and forgot to bring the tarot card reader his drink. As Montandon recounts in *The Intruders*, the card reader:

> … bolted to his feet with his curious retinue following suit, and explained loudly that he'd never been so insulted in his life. Quivering with rage he directed a stream of abuse at me: He had never been treated so rudely … I was an insufferable,

ungracious hostess … he was leaving, but not before he made certain I would never
have any happy moments in that house again. He fixed me with a glare, his face
puffed and distorted, "I lay a curse upon you and this house. I do not forget, and I
do not forgive. Remember that!

After the tarot card reader cursed her, Pat Montandon experienced a series of odd misfortunes. A chill encased the house, even though she cranked the thermostat to 90 degrees. Bloodstains appeared on the ceiling. Doors locked themselves. Vandals broke in. When Montandon authored the book *How to Be a Party Girl, TV Guide* mistakenly listed her show as "Pat Montandon: From Party Girl to Call Girl." Three of Montandon's friends died. Two committed suicide inside her house. On June 20, 1969, the master bedroom caught fire. When the fire department arrived, they found the front door and bedroom door barred from inside. Inside the house they discovered the body of Montandon's friend and secretary Mary Louise Ward. Her cause of death was never determined. According to the autopsy, she was already dead when the bedroom went up in flames …

Montandon finally hired ghost busters Gerri Patton and Nick Nocerino, who supposedly photographed the ghosts at 1000 Lombard. Though Nocerino performed an exorcism and declared the house safe, Montandon insisted on moving out.

Cursed by Satanists

The opulent Fox Theater once occupied the entire area bounded by Market, Hayes, and Polk streets. In 1963, real estate developers bought the property, demolished the Fox, and built an ugly high-rise. On the night of the Fox's last show, the organist—none other than Anton LaVey, future founder of the Church of Satan—cursed the property's owners. The high-rise has apparently suffered problems ever since and retains a creepy ambience that strengthens as the elevator lifts you to the upper floors.

San Francisco has only one drawback. 'Tis hard to leave.

– Rudyard Kipling

Reagan's War Record

During his presidency, Ronald Reagan claimed that he had fought in World War II. Though Reagan was a second lieutenant during the war, he never saw combat or even left the U.S. Instead, he worked a desk job, tracking lost packages in San Francisco's Fort Mason Building.

The Man Blamed For AIDS

The "patient zero" myth involves Gaëtan Dugas, an irresistibly handsome Canadian airline steward who brought HIV to San Francisco, California, or even North America, depending whom you read. Andrew R. Moss gives one of the most pernicious examples of this myth. When *California Magazine* published excerpts from Randy Shilt's book on AIDS, *And the Band Played On*, the magazine paid for a half-page ad in the *New York Times*. The ad displayed Dugas's photograph above a text beginning: "The AIDS epidemic in America wasn't spread by a virus. It was spread by a single man ... A Canadian flight attendant named Gaëtan Dugas ... " Mr. Dugas, who died in 1984, was not around to defend himself.

This myth is based on Auerbach and Darrow's 1984 study showing that 40 of the first 248 AIDS patients in the U.S. (diagnosed before April 1982) had either had sex with Dugas or with someone who had. The study places Dugas in the center of a diagram with his sex partners and their sex partners radiating out from him. Dugas clearly got around a lot. But the purpose of the diagram was to show that HIV was sexually transmitted, not that Dugas introduced HIV into the U.S., or that he was the first person diagnosed.

At the time of the study, the incubation period between HIV infection and AIDS was thought to be only one year. Dugas's partners in the study had sex with him, on average, 11 months before they developed AIDS. Now we know that the average incubation period is 10 years, so Dugas's partners almost certainly contracted the virus long before they slept with him.

The Aluminum Foil Cure

In recent years, people have expressed growing concern that the ELF (extra-low-frequency) radiation emitted by power lines, wiring, and electronic equipment (such as computers and televisions) may cause adverse health effects ranging from depression to increased risk of cancer. Studies are inconclusive, but some San Francisco residents are conducting research of their own.

In 1993, *Filth* magazine published a report claiming that the U.S. military was beaming ELF radiation at residents of San Francisco's Tenderloin. The author suspected that the Federal Building at 450 Golden Gate Avenue housed ELF transmitters. The military is experimenting with ELF because this type of radiation "[seems] to cause aberrations in the thought processes of human beings, such as hallucinations, disordered thought, confusion, aggression, depression, anger, hopelessness."

As evidence the author, who lived near the Federal Building, claimed that he had experienced symptoms of ELF on at least 15 occasions. The symptoms appeared when he heard a low buzz and observed its effect on other Tenderloin denizens: "An unusual number of fights could be heard breaking out all around me. From out on the streets, and from adjoining buildings, and apartments, came the shouts and threats of people overcome with anger." The author's most striking discovery was that he can block electromagnetic radiation and stop the buzz by wrapping his head in aluminum foil.

Rotting Flesh in Satanist's Yard

Anton LaVey founded the Church of Satan in San Francisco in 1966. He moved to 1198 Fulton Street and made himself at home. But the next year, LaVey's neighbors complained about his pet lion, Tagore, and the large bones and rotten flesh he left in LaVey's yard. When the city would no longer allow him to keep Tagore as a pet, LaVey donated the lion to the San Francisco Zoo. Oddly, most of the neighbors who had lodged complaints against Tagore died, moved away, or mysteriously vanished. Distraught at the loss of his pet, LaVey took drastic measures when the zoo director shipped Tagore to the Lion Country Safari near Los Angeles in 1968. According to Dr. Eldritch Weirde, the satanist performed a ritual involving an Egyptian crystal baboon. The next time the director entered the apes' cage at the zoo, the apes attacked and mauled him.

The Federal Vampire and Zombie Agency (FVZA)

The miners who came to northern California in the 1850s faced a range of discomforts, including rumored vampire sieges. The Federal Vampire and Zombie Agency reports on its Web site (www.fvza.org):

The Copper Creek Siege of 1855, in which vampires took over an entire California mining town, underscored the country's need for an organized, well-trained force to combat the growing plague. The Civil War delayed implementation until 1868, when President Ulysses S. Grant officially formed the Federal Vampire and Zombie Agency.

The myth of the siege has circulated around San Francisco for some time. In one version, bloodthirsty vampires stalked miners staggering home from the bars at night. Pouncing from behind trees, the vampires sunk their teeth into the miners' necks. They also stole the miners' gold and hid it in their underground coffins.

One of the Federal Vampire and Zombie Agency's most famous cases concerns the opium-addicted vampires in San Francisco's Chinatown. During the 1800s, Chinatown was virtually impenetrable to law enforcement due to the Tongs, organized crime gangs that operated opium dens, brothels, and gambling parlors. Jim Belmore, head of the Federal Vampire and Zombie Agency's San Francisco office, hired Chinatown native Jin Don Song to help him navigate this world. Jin Don thus became the first Asian-American FVZA agent.

Despite the long arm of the FVZA, seven vampires are currently rumored to reside in San Francisco. The vampire Lestat, whom Anne Rice chronicled in her best-selling book *Interview With A Vampire*, was said to have lived at 280

Divisadero Street. A sprawling and austere Victorian mansion with perpetually drawn shades now stands at this address. One of the authors of this book lives nearby. She confirms that the neighborhood retains a malevolent atmosphere of unseen evil—especially after dark when the fog rolls in. She remains wary of evening encounters with well-dressed young men who gaze fondly at her neck.

PART IV:
Oddballs & Weirdos

It is hardly fair to blame America for the state of San Francisco, for its population is cosmopolitan and its seaport attracts the floating vice of the Pacific; but be the cause what it may, there is much room for spiritual betterment.

— Sir Arthur Conan Doyle

I never saw so many well-dressed, well-fed, business-looking Bohemians in my life.

— Oscar Wilde on the San Francisco Bohemian Club

One person's madman is another person's eccentric. It's just a matter of interpretation. San Francisco has always had more than its fair share of weirdos. It's a city in which you have to be truly kooky to get noticed.

San Francisco's favorite oddball is Emperor Joshua Norton, a ruined gold rush speculator who declared himself Emperor of the United States and Protector of

Mexico. Norton issued his own currency, which local merchants honored. He even knighted the San Francisco city supervisors when they bought him a new uniform. When he died in 1880, the *San Francisco Chronicle* proclaimed, "*Le Roi Est Mort*," and flags flew at half-mast.

San Franciscans also adored freak show stars like Oofty Goofty and Big Bertha, who ornamented the Barbary Coast stage. Oofty Goofty made his first appearance as a "wild man from Borneo," covered in tar and horsehair. The costume wouldn't come off after the show and eventually he had to go to the hospital to have it removed. When the doctors couldn't peel off the tar and horsehair, they doused him with tar solvent and laid him out on the hospital roof to dry.

Oddball James Riley was the most famous of San Francisco's "hoodlums." He butted his opponents with his head and sold nude photos of himself to elegant courtesans, who displayed them prominently over their beds. Eccentric society lady Lillie Hitchcock Coit 5 was obsessed with fire fighting. Engine Company Knickerbocker No. 5 adopted her as their mascot—making her the nation's first fire woman. In her honor, the city built Coit Tower, which looks suspiciously like a 210-foot fire hose nozzle, though the architect swore that was not his intent.

The world-renowned San Francisco physician, Dr. Albert Abrams, pioneered the use of X rays for treating heart disease. But Abrams also founded 12 schools of Electronic Medicine based on strange instruments called the "biodynamometer" and "oscilloclast." He claimed these devices could cure any disease, foretell a patient's lifespan and exact time of death, transmute silver into gold, and detect an individual's religion.

Other local loons included lawyer Melvin Belli, who shot off a cannon and raised the Jolly Roger over his office on Montgomery Street every time he won a case. In court, during one of his many divorces, he referred to his wife as "El Trampo."

San Francisco's leading eccentric writer is Danielle Steel. The best-selling romance novelist lives in a mansion at 2080 Washington Street, where she often starts her drafts by typing 24 hours straight on a 1946 Olympia manual typewriter. Married and divorced five times, Steel seems to prefer dangerous types like the dashing men in her romance novels. To date, she has married a convicted bank robber and serial rapist, an ex-con heroin addict, and a shipping magnate who was convicted of manslaughter following a yachting incident in the south of France. She had nine children with these men and somehow has managed to write 61 best-selling books.

The Man Who Made a Fortune Buying Sand Dunes

James Lick was a hatchet-faced, skeletal man who came to Yerba Buena in 1847 and bought a bunch of worthless sand dunes behind a row of shacks and tents. The next year, the gold rush turned the tiny village into a boomtown, and the sand dunes became Montgomery Street. Though he owned more land than anyone else in San Francisco, Lick still wore the same shabby black suit and lived in the same rundown shack. At night, he slinked through the back alleys of the city and begged for bones from hotels and restaurants, which he ground up to fertilize his fruit orchards.

In the summer of 1874, Lick announced he was about to die. He appointed seven trustees to distribute his estate of three to four million dollars among a variety of organizations and philanthropic causes. Eight months later he felt much better, so he revoked his trust and established a new one with a new board of trustees. When the trustees sold some of his property to enact the second trust, Lick revoked this one as well and established a third with seven new trustees. He finally died in October 1876 at the astonishing age of 80. Most people of the late 1800s felt lucky if they lived to 50.

Lick's School of Mechanical Arts, Pioneers Monument, and a statue of Francis Scott Key in Golden Gate Park still stand. In his will, Lick requested that the sculptor of the Pioneers Monument place a farmer in the lead. The trustees and the sculptor pushed the farmer to the side and erected a miner in front.

Emperor of the United States and Protector of Mexico

On September 17, 1859, Joshua Abraham Norton proclaimed himself Emperor of the United States. A regal figure in a blue military uniform with gold epaulettes, a purple sash, a plumed beaver hat, and a sword, he presented the following edict to the *San Francisco Bulletin*:

> At the peremptory request and desire of a large majority of the citizens ... I, Joshua A. Norton, declare and proclaim myself Emperor of these United States ... [Signed] Norton I, Emperor of the United States and Protector of Mexico.

After Norton proclaimed himself emperor, he visited the banks and applied for million dollar loans under the title of Emperor of the United States. The banks politely refused. Unfazed, Norton printed his own currency—with the image of his face—in 10-, 25-, and 50-cent denominations. In other cities, people would have insisted Norton pay for things with real money. But San Francisco merchants accepted the bills graciously, as if they'd been using the wrong currency all along and their world was no more real than Norton's empire.

Perhaps Norton wasn't delusional, but he had simply found an easy way to make a living. His "madness" actually turned out to be his saving grace. By minting his own currency, he managed to escape from the financial world that had destroyed him, while other ruined speculators were driven to despair and shot themselves.

Norton died in 1880 on the corner of California and Grant Streets. The *San Francisco Chronicle* proclaimed, "*Le Roi Est Mort.*" Flags flew at half-mast, and 30,000 loyal subjects followed Norton's coffin to his grave. Even the deaths of his dogs, Bummer and Lazarus, occasioned citywide grief. Mark Twain penned a eulogy for Bummer, while a funeral procession honored Lazarus. Both dogs were stuffed and publicly displayed.

San Francisco still remembers Norton. He appears as a character in a local comic strip, and at least three current organizations—the Imperial Court of San Francisco, the Cacophony Society, and E Clampus Vitus—make yearly pilgrimages to his grave. There is also a movement afoot to rename the Bay Bridge after Emperor Norton, who issued an 1869 edict to build bridges across the bay to Oakland, Marin, and the Farallon Islands.

Oofty Goofty in a Cage

Oofty Goofty made his first appearance in a Market Street freak show as a "wild man from Borneo." To make his act more convincing, he covered his entire body in tar and horsehair. For a dime, people watched him devour raw meat, rattle the bars of his cage, and holler, "Oofty Goofty! Oofty Goofty!"—hence his stage name.

After his performance, Oofty Goofty spent several days in the Receiving Hospital. When the doctors couldn't remove the tar and hair without peeling off his skin, they doused him with tar solvent and laid him out on the hospital roof to dry.

After his unpleasant experience in the hospital, Oofty Goofty gave up freak show work and tried his skill as a singer and dancer. Bottle Koenig's beer hall allowed him to perform one song before they kicked him out on the stone sidewalk. Peeling himself off the sidewalk, Oofty Goofty realized he was insensitive to pain and could capitalize on this gift.

> *Oofty Goofty gave up freak show work and tried his skill as a singer and dancer.*

For the next 15 years, Oofty Goofty made a living charging people 10 cents to kick him, 25 cents to whack him with a cane, and 50 cents to pummel him with a baseball bat, which he carried for that purpose. He approached groups of men on the street with the invitation, "Hit me with a bat for four bits, gents? Only four bits to hit me with this bat, gents." Boxing champion John L. Sullivan finally fractured his spine with a billard cue—thus ending his career.

Queen of the Confidence Women

Barbary Coast historian Herbert Asbury describes Big Bertha as "a sprightly lass of 280 pounds who sang sentimental ballads in a squeaky soprano." She arrived in San Francisco in the mid 1880s, posing as a rich widow seeking a gentleman to look after her money. To test her suitors' mettle, she required applicants to hand over a sum of money, which she would double and risk on an undisclosed investment. Using this scam, she pocketed thousands of dollars.

By the time she was arrested, Big Bertha had achieved such widespread renown that none of her victims could face the public humiliation of suing her. Her case was dropped, and local melodeon owners Ned Foster and Jack Hallinan happily took her under joint management and charged 10 cents admission to see Big Bertha, the Queen of the Confidence Women. Before rapt audiences Bertha recounted her life of villainy, then burst into the only two songs she knew: *A Flower from My Angel Mother's Grave* and *The Cabin Where the Old Folks Died.*

Lillie Hitchcock Coit 5 and her Fire Fighting Fetish

In May 1851, San Francisco burst into flames. Seven-year-old Lillie Hitchcock and her family saw the blaze from a hundred miles away as they sailed up the California coast. The army had transferred Lillie's father to San Francisco. By the time they arrived, the blaze had subsided, but the city lay in ruins. Commerce ground to a halt and residents were living in tents amid the debris.

Several weeks later, Lillie had a more intimate encounter with fire. She and another little girl were playing at a construction site when a blaze broke out, trapping them inside the burning structure. A fireman from Knickerbocker Engine Company No. 5 chopped a hole in the roof, climbed inside, and carried them to safety.

From that moment on, Lillie was obsessed with fire fighting and particularly with Knickerbocker No. 5. When the fire bell rang, she would race after the engine and cheer on the firemen as they sprayed the flames. Eventually they let her ride on top of the fire truck. She wore the company badge and signed her name "Lillie Hitchcock 5" for the rest of her life. As an adult, she had the numeral 5 embroidered on her underwear.

Worried about their daughter's unusual interest, Lillie's high society parents sent her to a convent school in San Jose. Lillie missed Knickerbocker No. 5 so much she could barely eat. Her parents had to take her home before she wasted away.

Lillie's passion for fires only burned brighter as she grew up and became "the most dashing belle San Francisco ever knew," or the "queen of American society," as the Parisians said. San Francisco's elite loved and encouraged her zaniness. She attended a whirl of balls, galas, receptions, parties, and, of course, fires—which she treated almost like another social event. After a fire, she liked to take the soot-covered firemen out to dinner at a fine restaurant.

The delighted firefighters eventually presented her with a certificate of membership making her the nation's first woman to join a fire company. Her distraught parents exiled her to Calistoga. Finally, her parents gave up and let her stay in the city where she bought carpeting and curtains for the Knickerbocker No. 5 clubhouse, played poker, and smoked cigars with the firemen. She wore men's clothes, became an expert markswoman, attended illegal cockfights, and crashed men-only clubs.

When Lillie died in 1929 at age 87, the living members of Knickerbocker No. 5 made sure her "5" broach was pinned near her heart. They buried her in the Cypress Lawn Cemetery with a headstone inscribed "Lillie Hitchcock Coit 5." In her honor, the city built Coit Tower, which looks like a 210-foot fire hose nozzle, though the architect swears that was not his intent.

"Where else but in San Francisco would characters such as Sister Boom-Boom, a transvestite who dresses in a miniskirted nun's habit, and a punk rocker named Jello Biafra run for seats on the Board of Supervisors? And where else would 75,000 runners dress like centipedes, gorillas, and six packs of beer to participate in the 'moving masquerade ball' otherwise known as the Bay to Breakers Race?"

— JoAnne Davidson

Butt Riley: Hoodlum, Nude Model

The most famous of San Francisco's hoodlums was James Riley, also known as Butt Riley or King of the Hoodlums. Born around 1848 in New York, Riley came to San Francisco in 1868. Instead of fighting with his fists or another weapon, he took a running start and butted his opponent with his head. He once butted a 160-pound man 10 feet, and he charged 50 cents or a dollar to knock down doors.

The Barbary Coast courtesans adored Butt Riley. He boasted that they paid him for his services, and he supplemented his income by selling them photos of himself. Each Monday, Riley had new photographs taken and took them to the red-light district where he charged 25 cents or 50 cents per nude photo. Many of the city's most sought-after prostitutes displayed signed nude photos of Butt Riley over their beds.

The Crazy Speculator

Harry Meiggs was a well-meaning man who loved San Francisco and never intended to bankrupt the city. He built a house called the "Birdcage" on the Montgomery Street side of Telegraph Hill in the mid 1800s and served on a number of committees concerned with the growth of the city. Living in the Birdcage, Meiggs watched San Francisco grow in every direction except north. Telegraph Hill and Nob Hill seemed to stunt the city's northward expansion. So

Meiggs began buying property in the area he called North Beach and dreamed of extending the city northward all the way to the water.

With his own money, Meiggs built a North Beach pier that extended one-third of a mile into the bay. Everyone marveled. But Meiggs was ahead of his time. San Francisco wasn't ready for North Beach. The city was full of speculators who panicked at any hint of financial distress.

During the summer of 1854, when Meiggs finished North Beach, rumor spread that the stock market was about to crash. Nobody wanted to risk moving to North Beach. As the bills poured in Meiggs paid them as best he could, but soon he was bankrupt.

One day, Meiggs stopped by City Hall to see his brother John, who was the city comptroller. In his brother's office, he stumbled upon a book of blank checks. Each check was fully backed by the city treasury, and the mayor had already signed them so the comptroller wouldn't have to interrupt him for his signature. Meiggs reasoned he could use the checks until the eager investors bought up his beloved North Beach. Surely this would happen before the checks came due?

When North Beach hadn't picked up by autumn, Meiggs grew worried. He'd written hundreds of thousands of dollars in city checks. What to do? Finally, he approached a captain at Meiggs Wharf and bought a ship called the *American*. Meiggs paid for the ship with a city check, stocked it with food and supplies, and hastened his family on board for a cruise around the bay. On October 6, 1854, they sailed out the Golden Gate and into the Pacific—leaving behind their house, all of Meiggs' properties, more than $1,000,000 in debt, and $800,000 in embezzled city funds. Within four months, nearly half of San Francisco's banks had shut down.

George Washington the Second

Uncle Freddie Coombs, a phrenologist and George Washington impersonator, lived in San Francisco in the 1870s and 1880s. Though he already resembled the first president, he enhanced the effect by wearing a Continental army uniform, a powdered wig, knee breeches, and a tricorn hat. He also carried a large sign that identified him as "Washington the Second." Coombs appeared nightly at the Martin and Horton saloon with his state papers and maps. Believing the bar was the White House and General Headquarters, he planned military maneuvers and wrote letters to Congress and foreign nations. One winter he nearly starved to death, convinced he was at Valley Forge.

Cobweb Palace

Abe Warner opened his Cobweb Palace at Meiggs Wharf in 1856 and operated it until 1897, when he retired at age 80. Since Warner loved spiders and refused to injure their webs, cobwebs covered the inside of his saloon, from the walls and ceiling to the light fixtures and bottles of gin and whiskey behind the bar.

Ironically, Warner was also an art collector, though one could barely see his paintings of nudes beneath the cobwebs on the walls.

William Walker, the famous San Francisco soldier of fortune, frequented the Cobweb Palace during his years in San Francisco. Walker, who had no more compunction about invading spiders' webs than Latin American countries, once poked at a cobweb with his cane. According to local historian Herbert Asbury, "Warner remarked: 'That cobweb will be growing long after you've been cut down from the gibbet.' It was only about three years later that Walker was shot by a firing squad in Honduras."

The King of Pain

The King of Pain was a contemporary of Emperor Norton and a fellow street royal. Herbert Asbury calls him "the most ornate personage in the San Francisco of his time." He paraded through the streets of San Francisco dressed in velvet robes, scarlet underwear, and an ostrich plumed stovepipe hat, in a black coach drawn by six white horses. Unlike Norton, the King of Pain had a regular job as a patent-medicine salesman. He sold pain-relieving aconite liniment at Third and Mission, but lost his fortune gambling and killed himself. He lacked Norton's saving delusions.

The Great Unknown

In the 1860s, the Great Unknown, impeccably dressed with a gold-headed cane, walked Montgomery Street every afternoon. He resisted eye contact and spoke to no one. He remained a mystery for many years, until he finally hosted a public reception in Pacific Hall. For an admission fee of 25 cents a head, he revealed that he was a retired German tailor, William Frohm.

Dancers in Diapers

The Bull Run, also known as Hell's Kitchen and Dancehall, was one of the toughest dives on the Barbary Coast. It opened its doors at Pacific and Sullivan Alley in 1868. The owner, Ned "Bull Run" Allen, wore ruffled shirts and a rock-size diamond. He powdered his huge red nose with flour. Allen employed 40 or 50 women who wore diapers because they weren't allowed to leave the stage or dance floor—no matter how much they drank.

Happy Jack Inveighs against the Evils of Temperance

Happy Jack Harrington owned the Opera Comique on Murderer's Corner at the intersection of Jackson and Kearny Streets. He wore a wide-brimmed top hat, a white ruffled shirt, frock coat, skintight lavender pants, and a mustache "so long that he could tie its ends under his chin." In 1878, he succumbed to the appeals of the Praying Band, a women's temperance organization. Happy Jack sold his dive, but it wasn't more than a month before he was back in the Barbary Coast lecturing on the evils of temperance.

The Rich Girl Who Liked Asian Princes

All of San Francisco watched the amorous exploits of Aimée Crocker, a turn-of-the-19th-century tabloid figure. After inheriting $11 million and marrying two Americans, Crocker seduced a string of foreign royals, who apparently found her just as exotic as she found them. Missionaries pleaded with her to leave Hawaii, where she hosted orgies and swam every night with King Kalakua, who gave her an island near Molokai. Other flames included the chief shogun of Shanghai, the prince of Borneo, the

> *Crocker had serpents tattooed on her arms and owned two 12-foot boa constrictors.*

maharaja of Shikarpur, a raja of Calcutta, and two Russian princes. Her American and French husbands did not have titles. To Crocker's glee and her family's horror, the *San Francisco Chronicle* reported all her scandalous adventures, including a brief sojourn in a harem in India. Crocker had serpents tattooed on her arms and owned two 12-foot boa constrictors named Kaa and Prince Paul, who wound themselves around her as she slept. She enjoyed getting Oscar Wilde drunk in order to make him say "scandalous things." Having married five times, her full title when she died was Princess Aimée Crocker-Ashe-Gillig-Gourand-Miskinoff-Galitzine.

Ittzy Lives

Mrs. Dora Herz and her son Ittzy owned a store on the south side of Pacific between Montgomery and Sansome. They competed with another merchant, Solomon Levy, who owned a store half a block away and gave a sampling of his poetry to every customer who spent more than a dollar.

Ittzy was at a saloon on East Street when a Barbary Coast Ranger (or rogue) pulled a gun on him and claimed that Ittzy had sold him a bad pair of shoes. The Ranger fired, but the bullet whizzed past Ittzy and killed a bystander. Witnesses swore that "An unseen force had twitched the Ranger's hand just before he pulled the trigger. Thereafter for several weeks, so many people came to see Ittzy that his mother locked him in a back room and charged 10 cents to peek at him through a hole cut in the door."

Bierce's *Devil's Dictionary*

Ambrose Bierce was known as the "wickedest man in San Francisco." Born in Meigs County, Ohio, he remembered his mother and father as "unwashed savages." His friends he called "predictably idiotic."

President Theodore Roosevelt expressed interest in meeting Bierce, one of the most celebrated writers of his day. When they met, Roosevelt gave him a tour of the White House and showed him, with particular pride, the painting of the Rough Riders at San Juan Hill. When the president asked how he liked the painting, Bierce said he didn't like it: "It shows you at the heart of the action, whereas actually you weren't even there."

Bierce collaborated on a book called *The Dance of Death*, which condemned the waltz as "an open and shameless gratification of sexual desire and a cooler of burning lust." The book became a best-seller and was endorsed by the Methodist Church, which missed the point and wholeheartedly denounced the sin of waltzing.

Bierce is best known for his *Devil's Dictionary*, first published as a serial in the *San Francisco Illustrated Wasp*. A distinguished soldier in the Union army, Bierce decided to resume his military career at the age of 71. In 1913, he left for Mexico to join the forces of Pancho Villa. He was never heard from again.

Jack London's Mystery Father

When Jack London was eight months old, his mother married his stepfather, John London. Suspecting that John London was not his real father, 21-year-old Jack crossed the bay to the San Francisco Library and looked up "Flora Wellman Chaney," his mother's name, in the archives of the *San Francisco Chronicle*. He found this headline: "A Discarded Wife: Why Mrs. Chaney Twice Attempted Suicide … Driven from Home for Refusing to Destroy an Unborn Infant." The story—from June 4, 1875, six months before Jack's birth—described how his pregnant mother had downed laudanum then put a gun to her forehead when William H. Chaney, a struggling astrologer, had thrown her out and refused to give her money. The article suggested Chaney was the father, but left this open for doubt: Mr. and Mrs. Chaney "have been known for a year past as the center of a little band of Spiritualists, most of whom professed, if they did not practice, the offensive free-love doctrines of the licentious Woodhull."

William H. Chaney had left San Francisco in December 1875, but Jack found his address in Chicago. In response to Jack's letter, Chaney replied that he had never married Flora Wellman. He conceded that they had lived together, but claimed he was impotent at the time and thus could not be Jack's father. He suggested several other men who might be—a gentleman from Springfield, a broker, and a certain Lee Smith of Seattle. Most of London's biographers believe Chaney was, in fact, his father.

If you're alive, you can't be bored in San Francisco. If you're not alive, San Francisco will bring you to life.

— William Saroyan

A Consultation with Dr. Albert Abrams

When a patient consulted the world-renowned Dr. Albert Abrams at his San Francisco office in the early 1920s, the physician took samples of the patient's saliva, blood, and handwriting. A photograph supposedly worked as well. After treating the samples with a horseshoe magnet to remove "extraneous electronic emissions," Abrams placed the blood, saliva, and handwriting on a round plate called a "biodynamometer" or "dynamizer."

The doctor then summoned a healthy bare-chested laboratory assistant and treated him with the horseshoe magnet as well. After another assistant removed all red and orange materials from the room, the healthy subject stood facing west on two grounded metal plates. A series of rheostats linked an electrode on the subject's forehead to the dynamizer containing the patient's blood, saliva, and handwriting samples. Abrams would then tap the man's abdomen and recite a series of numbers, "28.5 ohms … 24.3 ohms," while an assistant took notes.

The inventor of these unorthodox procedures came from a conventional medical background. Albert Abrams (1863–1924) received his medical degree from the University of Heidelburg when he was only 20. Abrams' practice took an unusual turn around 1910. In 1917, he published his magnum opus, *Electronic Reactions of Abrams* (E.R.A.). According to the electronic theory of disease, the human body emitted electronic vibrations of a certain rate. Each disease caused a specific deviation in this rate of vibration. Abrams invented the dynamizer to measure these deviations and thus diagnose the patient.

Ahead of His Time

Jaime de Angulo (1887–1950), considered wildly eccentric in his day, anticipated many offbeat cultural explorations, from cross-dressing to shamanism and Native American studies. A Parisian-born Spaniard, de Angulo received his M.D. from Johns Hopkins University and also authored publications on linguistics and anthropology.

De Angulo cross-dressed like some of the Native American shamans he studied. His erotic interests in women's clothes predated his studies of California Indian culture. His daughter Gui wrote that in the 1930s, de Angulo, who lived in Big Sur, would dress in women's clothes and drive "to service stations out in the country, stop for gas and flirt with the service-station boys."

De Angulo also threw parties for transvestites and took estrogen to develop breasts long before other doctors began prescribing such substances for transsexuals. According to poet Robert Duncan, de Angulo often came to San Francisco in drag and seduced lesbians who "never discovered he was a man because his sexual activities were not of a kind that would display that little secret to them." Ekbert Faas writes, "Jaime's particular excursions into shamanistic male lesbian [transvestism] certainly confounded all traditional Western distinctions about gender." De Angulo would probably be considered transgender today.

Tattooed Tough Guy

Rasmus Nielsen started out as a blacksmith who worked in the mining camps north of San Francisco and got tattooed on the side for fun. His tattoos, drawn by "Brooklyn" Joe Lieber, included the Statue of Liberty under an eagle, a shield and flags on his back, Jesus faces on his ribs, and, on his legs, a Bill Cody portrait, geisha girls, dragons, and redwood trees.

When Nielson entered show business, the supply of tattooed men outweighed the demand. So he made a niche for himself by piercing his chest and lifting weights with the piercings. He worked up to lifting a 250-pound anvil clamped onto the rings in his chest. He also lifted weights with his tongue.

Billed as the "Tattooed Strongman" or "Tattooed Wonderman," Nielson worked with Ringling Bros. and Barnum & Bailey Circus from 1936 until 1948. He also worked for Robert Ripley's Believe it or Not Odditorium at the Golden Gate Exposition in San Francisco in 1940.

The Newspaper Mogul as a Young Man

Wealthy mine owner George Hearst acquired the eight-page *San Francisco Examiner* as repayment for a gambling dept. Hearst used the newspaper to promote his candidacy for the U.S. Senate. In 1887, after he won the election, he gave the paper to his 24-year-old son, William Randolph Hearst. William was thrilled. He sent reporters into emergency wards and insane asylums to dig up the most scandalous and sensational stories they could find. That year alone, circulation grew from 18,000 to 57,000.

The King of Torts

Lawyer Melvin Belli, known as the "King of Torts" or the father of modern personal injury law, represented Lenny Bruce, Errol Flynn, Zsa Zsa Gabor, Jack Ruby, Mae West, and the Rolling Stones. Each time he won a big case, he shot off a cannon and hoisted the Jolly Roger above his Montgomery Street office.

Belli went through six wives and 30 law partners during his 63-year career. These breakups were seldom peaceful. Belli once paid a $1,000 fine for dubbing his wife "El Trampo" in divorce court, and he trained his dogs to urinate and defecate outside his law partners' offices. He justified his behavior: "I was nothing until I became a screwball … When you're known, you're in a position to be listened to." He listed one of his dogs in the phone book as Weldone Rumproast.

The Purple Cow

Gelett Burgess is mostly remembered for his book *Goops and How to Be Them: A Manual of Manners for Polite Children*. In 1894, Burgess tore down a statue of Henry Cogswell, the temperance advocate who erected monuments of himself all over the city. This particular statue was highly visible—at the intersection of California and Market Streets. Burgess saw his act as homage to the revolutionary painter Gustave Courbet, who directed the demolition of Napoleon's column at the Place Vendôme during the Paris Commune. But Burgess's highbrow vandalism cost him his teaching job at the University of California at Berkeley.

Then in 1895, Burgess cofounded *The Lark*, a San Francisco-born modernist magazine that was so cutting edge that the *New York Times* described it as "incredibly, even impossibly, 1895." The first issue of *The Lark* published Burgess's poem:

I never saw a Purple Cow
I hope I never see one
But I can tell you anyhow
I'd rather see than be one.

Two years later the magazine's final issue (*The Epi-Lark*) published Burgess's retraction:

Ah, yes, I wrote the 'Purple Cow'
I'm sorry, now, I wrote it;

But I can tell you anyhow

I'll kill you if you Quote it!!

The Little Frog Catcher and Her Girl Gang

Even 19th-century San Francisco saw alliances between outlaw women. Jeanne Bonnet, or the Little Frog Catcher, was a woman who wore men's clothes and worked catching frogs in the San Mateo marshes. In the mid 1870s, she frequented the peep shows at Madame Johanna Werner's elegant parlor house on Sacramento Street. By early 1876, the Little Frog Catcher persuaded a dozen girls to leave the parlor houses and form a girl gang specializing in shoplifting and robbery. They established their headquarters in a shack by the water south of Market. Later that year, a pimp whose girls had run off with the gang shot the Little Frog Catcher through the heart. She was only 25.

Vatican Roulette

In 1958, the controversial Dr. James Pike became bishop of California's Episcopal Diocese. Supervising the completion of Grace Cathedral in downtown San Francisco, Pike added a stained-glass image of astronaut John Glenn to the more traditional depictions of saints. He riled the Catholic Church by calling the rhythm method of Pope-sanctioned birth control "Vatican roulette."

The Poet Who Made Mist Rise

In 1948, Helen Adam moved to San Francisco with her mother and sister. Born in Glasgow, Scotland, in 1909, Adam had been hailed as a child prodigy because she spoke in rhyme to her dolls. At 14, she published *The Elfin Peddler*, composed of 120 ballads she had written since the age of two. In San Francisco, Adam wrote plays, including *Initiation to the Magic Workshop* and *San Francisco's Burning*, which appeared on Broadway. Most of her work focused on witchcraft, ritual, and ancient folklore. The beats called her the "Godmother of the San Francisco Renaissance." Legend has it that her voice made mist rise when she chanted her poems. She died in 1992.

The Silent Beat

Robert Garnell "Bob" Kaufman, African-American beat poet and cofounder of *Beatitude* magazine, took a Buddhist vow of silence after witnessing the assassination of John F. Kennedy. He did not speak for 10 years, until the end of the Vietnam War. In 1978 he resumed silence and seldom spoke until his death in 1986.

Would-Be Assassins Wear Bicentennial Blouses

On September 23, 1975, former FBI informant Sara Jane Moore fired a .38-caliber pistol at President Gerald Ford as he left the Westin St. Francis Hotel in

Union Square. Only 17 days earlier, Manson family member Lynette "Squeaky" Fromme had aimed a gun at Ford in Sacramento. Both Moore and Fromme received life sentences. On November 8, 1976, *Newsweek* described Fromme's wardrobe selections in the San Diego Metropolitan Correctional Center: "Along with her fellow inmates, she wears a pants outfit with a choice of blouses—one which is a Bicentennial print adorned with Liberty Bells, Revolutionary War soldiers, and fife-and-drum bandsmen."

Most Famous Twins

Marian and Vivian Brown, San Francisco's most famous twins, walk around the Financial District and Union Square sporting identical hairstyles and matching hats and dresses from the 1940s. Since moving to San Francisco in 1973, the twins have appeared in ads for IBM, Reebok, and Southwest Airlines, as well as a 1995 Joe Boxer underwear ad in New York's Times Square. Now "ladies of a certain age," the well-dressed twins playfully wink at you when you encounter them strolling around town.

> Now "ladies of a certain age," the well-dressed twins playfully wink at you.

Danielle Steel: Five Ex-Husbands, Nine Children, and 61 Best-Selling Books

Best-selling romance novelist Danielle Steel lives in a mansion at 2080 Washington Street at Octavia. Her life story rivals her novels in soap opera-style drama. She has married five times and raised nine children, one of whom died of a heroin overdose after a long struggle with bipolar disorder. Born in 1947, Steel survived childhood cancer and polio to graduate from New York's Lycée Français at 15. As an 18-year-old debutante, she married international banking scion Claude-Eric Lazard. After leaving Lazard, Steel was drawn to San Francisco where actor and conscientious objector Bruce Neckels was completing his prison sentence as a test subject for NASA. While visiting Neckels in the U.S. Public Health Service Hospital, she met convicted bank robber and serial rapist Danny Zugelder.

Though Steel claims he concealed his past, Zugelder says they discussed it, and it was the "ultimate thrill" for Steel to be with a convicted felon. When Zugelder was released from prison, his parole officer permitted him to live with Danielle in San Francisco. Things began to deteriorate when a pimp suggested Danny look after a prostitute who turned out to be 16 years old. Zugelder had already been convicted for raping a different teenager. Within the next few months, he was arrested for stealing an old woman's purse and then again for rape. Zugelder went back to prison, and—after all this—Steel married him in 1975.

Two years later, Steel divorced Zugelder to marry Bill Toth, a heroin addict and ex-con she had hired to help her move house. Husbands four and five included a venture capitalist and a shipping magnate who had been convicted of manslaughter following a yachting accident in the south of France. Her most recent relationship is with actor George Hamilton.

With so many children and ex-husbands, one wonders how Steel has found time to write her 61 best-selling romance novels. Her Web site says, "In the heat of a first draft, it is not uncommon for her to spend 18 to 20 hours a day glued to her 1946 Olympia manual typewriter." Readers spend more than $25 million a year on her books.

E Clampus Vitus

A men's club founded during the gold rush, E Clampus Vitus is unsure whether it is a "historical drinking society," or a "drinking historical society." Clampers, dressed in red mining shirts from the gold rush, research and dedicate plaques to ghost towns, saloons, brothels, soiled doves, madmen, and other people and places more traditional historians might overlook. Each year, they visit the grave of Emperor Norton, a ruined gold rush millionaire who proclaimed himself emperor.

Since the order's inception, members have maintained that all Clampers are "of equal indignity, but some, such as the Clampatriarch and the Noble Grand

Humbug, [are] more equal than others." The society's declared purpose is "to comfort widows and orphans—especially the widows."

The Woman With The Taped Nose

In the 1970s, a 5-foot-tall Irishwoman who lived in the Tenderloin district wore a piece of cellophane tape on her nose every day. The tape, which stretched from her upper lip to the crown of her head, made her nose resemble a pig's snout. When asked, she said she wore the tape so people would leave her alone.

The Red Man

The Red Man—a wizened Salvador Dali look-alike with black hair and a long cartoonish mustache—has painted his entire body red for the last 20 or 30 years. He can often be seen pushing his shopping cart around the Mission district. Once a denizen of Café Picaro at 16th and Mission Streets, he now frequents the Latin American Club at 3286 22nd Street, where he distributes wacky art made using a photocopy machine.

San Francisco beats the world for novelties; but the inventive faculties of her people are exercised as a specialty . . . Controversy is our forte.

— *San Francisco Call*, 1864

Scarlot Harlot

Some people will tell you that prostitution ended in San Francisco with the Red Light Abatement Act and collapse of the Barbary Coast in 1917. But one of today's most visible prostitutes is a fire-haired woman named Carol Leigh, aka Scarlot Harlot. Leigh began working as a prostitute in 1977, after graduate study at Boston University. More than a career change, it was a conversion experience. Since 1977, Leigh has agitated in the streets and on TV for the decriminalization of prostitution and made it her mission "to glorify sex workers" everywhere. She often appears in a headdress and floor-length skirt made from American flags.

San Francisco's Most Dedicated Protester

Dressed in professional business attire and heavy-duty sunglasses, Frank Chu commutes daily from Oakland to San Francisco where he walks the streets of Union Square carrying a protest sign. Chu protests Presidents Bush, Clinton, Jefferson, Buchanan, Van Buren, and 12 galaxies that are allegedly blocking his royalty checks from a TV show called *The Richest Family*.

He changes his sign frequently to correspond with his protest target. It may read, "Impeach Bush/ 12 Galaxies / Guiltied to / Omegalogical / Theoretical Analysis," or "Impeach Van Buren / 12 Galaxies / Guiltied to / Zegnatronic / Rocket Stations." He also sells the back of his sign to local businesses for $25 a week, undercutting billboard rents, at roughly $100 a day in San Francisco.

San Franciscans are so supportive of Mr. Chu and his causes that he now has an online presence. Fans have dedicated several Web sites to Chu, the 12 Galaxies and Zegnatronic Rocket Society. (See http://www.whack.org/~skott/guiltied.html and http://www.12galaxies.20m.com)

Mrs. Suzy Chu, presumably Frank's wife, posts messages on a popular mailing list, keeping his followers up-to-date on his daily routines. She writes, "When he comes home, I have dinner ready for him. A hotdog wrapped in aluminum foil (which he eats) and a packet of astronaut ice cream. Then its the same thing. He wraps himself in saranwrap and gets in his Mighty Mouse sleeping bag, turns on the plant lights, puts on his tanning goggles, and goes to sleep listening to the Partridge Family on the hifi."

Outlaw Women

San Francisco has a long history of attracting sexually rebellious women. Though the Barbary Coast collapsed in 1917 when the brothels closed, the cops still tolerated visible adult commerce, which drew tourists and buttressed the city's economy. The ladies and gentlemen of the night simply went underground, forming a secret outlaw society. Prostitutes hung out in particular bars and relied on bartenders who benefited from their business and protected them from the police and other hostile outsiders. A bartender might use a code word, abruptly change the music, or flash the lights to indicate the presence of an undercover cop. When lesbian bars began to open in North Beach, lesbians relied on the same relationships with bartenders and the same kinds of signals to make the bars safer for their communities.

There isn't much evidence of lesbian bars in San Francisco prior to 1933, but after Prohibition, lesbian culture flourished alongside and within the vice district's bawdy houses and dance halls. Like other sexual outlaws in San Francisco, lesbians shielded themselves from police harassment by performing and providing entertainment for tourists. Mona's, San Francisco's first lesbian nightspot, opened in 1934 and moved to Columbus Avenue in 1936. Through the rest of the 1930s and 1940s, more lesbian bars opened around Broadway and Montgomery in North Beach. As lesbians began to occupy public spaces, they became visible to the police as a deviant social group.

In this sense, lesbians followed the path of prostitutes, who had been visible in San Francisco since Latin American harlots pitched their tents on the southeastern slopes of Telegraph Hill during the first year of the gold rush. In the 1930s, lesbians began to take advantage of the protections surrounding the vice district in the same way that prostitutes did. Since women had few job options in the early twentieth century, lesbians often partnered with prostitutes or worked as prostitutes or pimps. The police sometimes confused lesbians with prostitutes and arrested them under antiprostitution laws. On September 21, 1956, the cops raided a lesbian hangout called Kelly's and charged 34 women with "frequenting a house of ill-repute." Though most of the women weren't working as prostitutes, they pleaded guilty as they viewed themselves as sexual outlaws.

Jello Biafra

Punk spoken-word artist Jello Biafra, born Eric Boucher in Boulder, Colorado, was a politically precocious child. After his father explained the Cuban missile crisis to him, Biafra started loud political arguments with his conservative grade school teachers. Later he moved to San Francisco to join the other activists. Living at 412 Clayton Street, he took acting classes by day and played in punk bands at night. Biafra formed the acclaimed punk band the Dead Kennedys and sang memorable tunes like *Holiday in Cambodia*. In 1979, Biafra formed the Alternative Tentacles record label to release Dead Kennedys albums. That year, he also ran for mayor of San Francisco. His platform included the provision that if elected, he would force businessmen to wear clown suits.

The Dead Kennedys' 1985 album *Frankenchrist* included a poster of H. R. Giger's artwork *Penis Landscape*. In response, the police raided Biafra's apartment on charges that the artist

> *Biafra started loud political arguments with his grade school teachers.*

was "distributing harmful matter to minors." Jello fought the charges and was acquitted after a long trial. After the Dead Kennedys broke up, he went on to pursue spoken word projects and more deliriously strange art.

Lawyer Creates Havoc

In 1993, the California Bar Association suspended Berkeley attorney Morgan Doyle for a series of incidents dating from 1985. First, Doyle allegedly fired a gun from his roof to honor the "exploration of the West" as a battleship sailed into San Francisco harbor. Another incident took place at a restaurant in 1991. Doyle demanded free croissants then threw food, threatening the owner and his wife when they refused his request. The bar association suspended Doyle for only 30 days because these incidents did not involve what they considered "moral turpitude."

Plaintiff Charges World Leaders, Movie Stars, Talk Show Host, Street Gangs, and Aliens with Harassment

In February 1994, a federal court in California dismissed a harassment complaint against the *San Francisco Chronicle*. The plaintiff had also filed harassment charges against 24 other defendants, including President George H.W. Bush, "the Queen of England," French President Mitterrand, "the founders of Israel," H. Ross Perot, the director of the FBI, several street gangs in Hong Kong, Phil Donahue, Kirk Douglas, Dennis Hopper, Paul Newman, Frank Sinatra, "the drug cartel," Oliver North, and a "humanoid alien extraterrestrial leader speaking Greek."

A Garbled Will

In 1995, across the bay from San Francisco, a Marin County judge probated the will of Sam Zakessian, who bequeathed $2 million to his girlfriend instead of to his family. The deceased left his instructions on a four-by-four-inch scrap of paper, which seemed to contain layers upon layers of scribblings. The court determined that this palimpsest included "Mr. Zakessian's initials written 21 times (some rotated, some sideways, some upside-down), three different dates (one sideways over three lines of text), and two signatures written diagonally." In February 1997, a California Court of Appeal upheld the lower court's ruling—conceding that Mr. Zakessian's will "is not easily described."

Man Kidnaps Himself

In July 1992, Russell C. Sultan phoned his mother and girlfriend, claiming he had been kidnapped, and begged them to pay his captors $23,000 in ransom. Tracing the phone calls to a motel room, San Francisco police surrounded the locked door and burst inside, guns drawn. Sultan, who was eating fried chicken and watching a 49ers football game, said his abductors had gone out for a bit. He asked the police, "What took you so long?" They arrested him on charges of extortion.

Homeless Woman Sues Restaurant

Through most of 1996, the Garden Juice Bar in San Francisco gave free meals to a homeless woman named Eugenia McCoy. But in January 1997, McCoy filed a complaint with the state labor department, claiming that the restaurant had not paid her for a year of 40-minute shifts standing outside to protect its windows from vandalism. The labor official scheduled a formal hearing, though the owners of the Garden Juice Bar denied that McCoy worked for them.

Thieves Steal Costume Jewelry

In November 1992, two thieves burst into Ciro, one of several jewelry boutiques lining a fashionable block of San Francisco's Post Street. The robbers thrust a sack at the clerk and ordered her to fill it with jewelry. "Why?" asked the clerk, stuffing baubles into the bag. On a block of expensive jewelers, Ciro was the one shop that sold only costume jewelry. The thieves made their getaway with a bulging sack of fake trinkets.

Eye on Crime

In 1986, San Francisco resident Kevin L. Hoover was reading *National Lampoon*'s "True Facts" column when he glimpsed his vocation in an excerpt from the *Arcata Union* newspaper: "Tiffany's ice cream parlor alerted police to a person defacing the statue of William McKinley on the Arcata Plaza. Police apprehended a suspect and released him with a warning not to stick cheese in McKinley's ears and nose anymore."

Hoover threw down the *National Lampoon* and, with light bulbs flashing in his brain, flew to Arcata, more than 200 miles north of San Francisco. In 1993, the *Arcata Union* hired him to author the "cop log." When the *Union* folded, Hoover launched the weekly *Arcata Eye*, which celebrated its eighth anniversary in October 2004.

In the *Arcata Eye*, Hoover narrates police escapades with poetic license. The police "have to say 'suspect exhibited erratic behavior,' when the truth might be that the guy was dyed green, wearing a bath towel, running down the street playing bagpipes," explains Hoover. The *San Francisco Chronicle* gives the following examples from Hoover's book, *The Police Log: True Crime & More from Arcata, California*, self-published by the *Arcata Eye*:

Oct. 30, 2001, 6:41 A.M.: One had a hat, one a hood / And both were way up to no good / Four cars fell to ravage / Now were they just savage / Or lonely and misunderstood?

Aug. 24, 2000, 1:19 A.M.: The delicate fluorescent ambiance of a 24-hour doughnut shop was either shattered or enhanced, depending on your perspective, by a public he-she frisson. The feuding fuss-budgets took their leave.

Sept. 8, 2000, 1:38 P.M.: Cows made it out of their pasture onto Bayside Cutoff, but proved too stupid to take their liberation from enslavement any further.

Jan. 22, 2001, 3:19 P.M.: The sound of that bongo was like a searing needle plunged into the cerebellum of a Plaza business-person. The artist ceased his bonking and left.

Nov. 16, 2001, 1:05 P.M.: A man at the front counter said / An antenna's been placed in his head / Is it yours? he asked cops / And with that, wandered off / To get back, one would hope, on his meds.

Are You Eccentric Enough?

In San Francisco, the competition is fierce for who is considered particularly eccentric. In 1995, Herb Caen, daily columnist for the *San Francisco Chronicle*, criticized a new book's selection:

You'd think dear old Kookville-by-the-Bay would be represented heavily in a new book published in England to a front-page rave in the London Sunday Times *book section — but nope. The book, titled* Eccentrics, *gives passing mention to Emperor Norton and Lillie Hitchcock Coit, but the only living S.F. eccentric listed is Gary Holloway, for two reasons: He founded the Martin Van Buren Fan Club "because he was the only president without a society," and he sometimes dresses as St. Francis of Assisi because "the habit is nice-looking and comfortable, and people always offer me a seat on the bus." Pretty tame stuff, if you ask me. Bring back Sister Boom-Boom. The noneccentric Gary Holloway, by the way, is on the staff at the Academy of Sciences in the Park.*

Sister Boom-Boom (aka Jack Fertig) was a longtime member of the Sisters of Perpetual Indulgence, a now-worldwide organization of drag nuns founded in San Francisco. These nuns (described in Part V) combine traditional habits with highly unconventional colorful white-face makeup, and a rocket-shaped wimple headdress known as "ear brassieres." Holloway, who merely wears a monk's frock, doesn't hold a candle to them.

Artist Sells Homeless Man

In November 1996, San Francisco's Museum of Modern Art featured the exhibit *Roger* by British artist Tony Kaye, 43. *Roger* is a homeless man who sits in a cube, where museum patrons can observe him and ask him questions. Prior to the exhibit, the homeless man, whose real name is Roger, signed a contract allowing Kaye to sell *Roger* as an artwork. "I know that Tony wouldn't sell me unless he knew I had a good home," Roger explained.

The Zippy Campaign

In May 2001, the *San Francisco Chronicle* sparked fury by dropping "Zippy the Pinhead" from their funny pages. Outraged readers demanded the restoration of the bald, pointy-headed antihero, and more than 200 fans—some dressed as pinheads—rallied in front of the *Chronicle*'s headquarters. The paper said they'd bring Zippy back only if they received 2,000 letters, the number of complaints the *L.A. Times* received when they pulled the comic strip, "Rex Morgan M.D." "Who knew that the careers of Zippy and Rex were so intertwined?" asked a Zippy devotee.

Ten-Foot Doggie Gets Nose Job

On April 1, 2001, a 10-foot, 700-pound fiberglass dachshund head tumbled off its rusty pole and plunged into Sloat Boulevard, shattering its nose. Shelby Foote and Scott Shankland saw the dog fall around 8:30 P.M. while driving eastbound on Sloat.

"It was so weird. I thought, 'What the hell is this thing flying through the air?'" said Shankland.

"It was quite the drama," Foote added. "There it was, falling to the ground. I said, 'Oh my God! It's the Doggie Diner head!'"

The large fiberglass object was in fact the last standing dog head that was once a symbol of the Doggie Diner, a San Francisco Bay Area fast-food chain that went out of business in 1986. The Doggie Diner is now another restaurant, but those who have loved the Doggie since 1966 cannot let go. When a public works crew hauled the Doggie off to a maintenance yard, concerned citizens rushed to the scene and demanded that his smiling snout be restored. A local newspaper columnist launched a campaign, and city supervisors finally earmarked $15,000 for repairs. Fans raised an additional $10,000 to get the pup back up.

After several months of painstaking care and a new nose job, the Doggie returned to the top of its pole on the corner of 46th Avenue and Sloat. The public rededication ceremony included local artist Anna Conti, who has exhibited a series of Doggie paintings, and John Law, the owner of three 700-pound Doggie heads that he carts around the city to various events. Law founded the "dogminican order" of San Francisco's First Church of the Last Laugh in honor of his Doggies.

Butts for Jesse

In January 1996, the San Francisco Bay Area's Society of Smoking Artists (SSA) launched the "Butts for Jesse" campaign. A totem of the far right, Republican Senator Jesse Helms supported tobacco subsidies while strongly opposing federal funding for the arts. Noting that "a very large percentage of artists are addicted to tobacco," the SSA asked "all smoking artists and art lovers who smoke to save their cigarette butts and send them to Senator Jesse Helms on a weekly basis."

The SSA hoped that Helms "might gain a greater appreciation for artists," when he learned that "as a demographic group, artists consume higher than average levels of cigarettes." Unfortunately, Helms remained curmudgeonly opposed to the arts, despite the SSA's noble efforts.

Little Black Dress Run

Though San Francisco's Castro district shimmers with drag queens on Friday and Saturday nights, running in drag is still considered a bit unusual—or at least uncomfortable, especially in stiletto heels. Yet once a year, the San Francisco FrontRunners, a gay and lesbian running club, don their frippery and go for a jog.

Dave Ford's description of the annual "Little Black Dress Run" in the *San Francisco Chronicle* sounds less like a run than a runway. Robert Miller of the Presidio district wears a "homemade headdress constructed with wire hangers and three feathered boas. Costume jewelry, a thrift-store black dress, and stack-heeled shoes complete the ensemble. His goatee is dyed blue, matching his blue glitter eyeshadow … Bob Callori looks fashionable in a paisley gold lamé skirt, with a matching handbag and a black top. A black shawl made from a laptop computer cover drapes his shoulders. His right hand holds a feather fan." Even a few local elected officials come out to jog. "San Francisco Supervisor Bevan Dufty looks svelte in a black miniskirt."

Like numerous other gay and lesbian organizations, FrontRunners started in San Francisco then spread around the world. The Web site (www. SFFrontRunners.org) calls FrontRunners "a world-wide network of running clubs for the LGBT community and our friends."

I have always been rather better treated in San Francisco than I actually deserved.

— Mark Twain

The Mad Piper

If you see a bald freak in a kilt playing the bagpipes on a street corner in San Francisco, it's probably bagpiper extraordinaire Ryan McCabe. According to his Web page [http://www.culannshounds. com/madpiper.htm], the Mad Piper studied at the Piping Center in Glasgow, Scotland, and the Academy of Piping in Maryland. He plays more than 60 shows a year and is currently single. The page encourages readers to "Hire the Mad Piper to play at your wedding, funeral, or scare away in-laws, exterminate pests, or get your Pictish hoard into a battle frenzy."

Red Dress Run

If you are straight, single, and looking for love, you might try the annual "Red Dress Run," sponsored by the San Francisco chapter of the Hash House Harriers, a frat-like organization that describes itself as "a drinking club with a running problem." The group guzzles beer before, after, and during their runs.

> *The group guzzles beer before, after, and during their runs.*

"Before the race," writes Nate Cavalieri for the *SF Weekly*, "balding businessmen hop out of their luxury sedans dressed in red sequins and feathers. A couple help their little boy wiggle into a red velvet Kewpie doll outfit. Two college-age girls turn up with a scaffolding of cherry fishnets climbing up from their sneakers." The group is "dedicated to vulgar traditions, chaotic disorganization, and 'hashes,' events that are equal parts footrace, frat house kegger, and scavenger hunt." Hashers also tend to pair off. The San Francisco chapter averages four or five weddings a year.

ArtCar Fest

A van covered with hundreds of disposable cameras and a hearse capped with a large black Gothic cathedral drove to San Francisco in September 2004 for the West Coast's largest convergence of art cars. Several modified motorcycles also participated, including a large furry cow named Cowasaki and a large yellow vehicle dubbed the Banana Bike. Art curator John Beardsley called the exhibit of heavily decorated, roadworthy vehicles the "quintessential public art of our time."

Life-Size Game of Mouse Trap

Remember Mouse Trap— the board game with mechanical gadgets and chain reactions, where you tried to capture your opponent's mouse before he caught yours? Mouse Trap isn't just for kids anymore. A group of San Francisco artists have built a "life-size" Mouse Trap, featuring wheels, gears, and mechanisms that smash a 500-pound pumpkin with a two-ton bank safe.

Tourists Report Shark Attacking Seal

A group of alarmed tourists called the San Francisco police after a shark emerged from the water and snagged a seal basking in the sun off Pier 39. The cops showed up at the scene, but the shark had not committed murder, kidnapping, or even cannibalism, and law enforcement could do little to stop the food chain in action.

The Little Poo Angel

The Little Poo Angel is a sweet fairy-godmother-like creature who comforts people hospitalized with intestinal problems. She wears an oblong-shaped gold lamé costume with little wings and a wand. The poo fairy dances, sings, and works hard to cheer people up. She now owns a bar in San Francisco and produces cultural events.

The Cyclecide Bike Rodeo: "Too Dumb to Die"

Founded in 1996, the Cyclecide Rodeo is a "touring punk rock bicycle amusement park" for cyclists who like welding, loud music, and rough riding. The group creates modified bicycles or "Alter-cycles," such as the fire-breathing Chupacabra bike and a tall bike made of two frames welded together.

With these Alter-cycles, the troupe of musicians, clowns, and general nutcases tour the country, sometimes providing entertainment at corporate events for companies like Bank of America. They perform stunts most riders would never attempt, including a tall bike joust and a bicycle mosh pit. The rodeo also offers dangerous bicycle rides such as the Whirl and Hurl, a pedal-propelled seesaw that spins violently in circles. Clowns add to the general chaos by taking pies in the face and shooting onlookers with beer from pressurized water pistols. The group's motto is "Too dumb to die!"

Herb Caen and Strange de Jim: The Man Behind the Pillowcase

From 1939 until his death in 1997, Herb Caen penned a daily column for the *San Francisco Chronicle*. *Chronicle* reporter Dave Ford said, "Caen's item-heavy pieces served both as a social clearinghouse and repository of the city's image as a sophisticated small town peopled with colorful characters."

One character who appeared regularly in Caen's column was a goofball known only as "Strange de Jim." From the 1970s through the 1990s, Caen peppered his daily observations with more than 300 quotes from Strange. Many fans thought Strange de Jim was an offshoot of Caen's imagination, but he was a real person who mailed Caen quips. Caen first cited Strange on September 17, 1972, after Strange sent him the following question: "Since I didn't believe in reincarnation in any of my other lives, why should I have to believe in it in this one?"

Strange later enhanced his mystique by appearing on a local TV show with a pillowcase with cutout eyeholes over his head. He then launched a series of "Strange de Luncheons" at a North Beach hangout called Enrico's. The guests wore pillowcase headgear in imitation of their host's trademark style. "Even Caen wasn't sure Strange existed," writes Ford for the *Chronicle*, "The two met only once, at a writers' conference in Santa Barbara in the early 1980s." They so enjoyed their epistolary relationship that they preferred not to meet up.

In the mid 1970s, Strange de Jim lived in Pacific Heights. Though he worked as an accountant, he began practicing massage as an experiment in trust. The massage client would arrive at Strange's home blindfolded. Strange would guide the person to his massage table and give an hour-long massage. Based on these trust exercises, Strange wrote and self-published *The Strange Experience* (1980)—a book that "set out his philosophy of how to attract people through the bonds of trust." Strange had previously self-published *Ha! I Made Herb Caen and I Can Break Him* (with an introduction by Herb Caen) and a New Age self-help book titled *Visioning*. But just before *The Strange Experience* went to press, Strange got cold feet. Rifling through the manuscript, he replaced the word "friend"—as in, "lead your new friend to the massage table"—with "victim." Strange believes this sabotaged the book's sales, but *Visioning* sold an impressive 20,000 copies.

More recently, Strange de Jim authored *San Francisco's Castro* (Arcadia Publishing, 2003), a black-and-white photo book that traces the history of the city's Castro district, a one-time Irish Catholic neighborhood that became the epicenter of gay rights in the 1970s. Strange has lived in the Castro since 1979.

When Herb Caen died in February 1997, Strange de Jim spoke at his funeral. In honor of the columnist, he removed the pillowcase from his head and announced, "I'm Just Plain Strange." Strange de Jim still writes under his nom de plume and prefers not to reveal his name.

Strange de Jimisms

In his daily column for the *San Francisco Chronicle*, Herb Caen quoted Strange de Jim more than 300 times. Here are some favorite quips from Jim's Web site:

By law you have to turn your headlights on when it's raining in Florida. To which Strange de Jim replies, "All right, but who's going to let me know it's raining in Florida?"

"Last week I really got burnt," admits Strange de Jim. "I went to a discount massage parlor, and it turned out to be self-service."

At the next table a diner produced a cigarette and asked Strange de Jim, "Do you mind if I give myself cancer?" "Certainly not," replied Strange, "as long as you don't smoke while you're doing it."

Strange de Jim at the Old Poodle Dog: "I won't eat snails—I prefer fast food."

"Monogamous," says Strange de Jim, "is what one partner in every relationship wants it to be."

The Cockettes

"Onstage, it's pandemonium: A sea of bodies writhes in an elaborate tangle of velvet, lace, baubles, and exposed flesh. The makeup is fabulous and the chests are hairy as men, women, and indefinables warble show tunes, sometimes even on key," writes *San Francisco Chronicle* reporter Carla Meyer, describing The Cockettes.

A "groundbreaking, gender-bending performance troupe," The Cockettes staged midnight musicals at the Palace Theater in San Francisco's North Beach from 1969 to 1972. The group, founded by "Hibiscus," a member of the KaliFlower commune, included gay men, women, and babies dressed in drag and way too much glitter. David Weissman, director and producer of The Cockettes' documentary, says that the troupe "symbolically ... defined the cusp—from the 1960s to the '70s—from the Haight-Ashbury psychedelic, hippie era into the beginnings of the sexual revolution and gay liberation." One of the troupe's best-known pieces is *Tricia's Wedding*, a film-spoof on the nuptials of President Nixon's daughter Tricia. Eartha Kitt, played by a man in drag, spikes the punch, triggering a mass orgy.

> A groundbreaking, gender-bending performance troupe

Though madly popular in San Francisco, The Cockettes did not fare as well in New York. Nationally syndicated columnist Rex Reed proclaimed The Cockettes "a landmark in the history of new, liberated theater" after he attended a San Francisco performance. "But the freewheeling, anarchic, atmosphere that so electrified the San Francisco shows didn't carry over to The Big Apple," writes Weissman. "The opening night throng of celebrities and socialites were bewildered by The Cockettes' seeming indifference to 'professionalism.' The press hated them, and the audience walked out in droves."

Nonetheless, The Cockettes garnered an underground following. According to Weissman, they inspired "the glitter rock era of David Bowie, Elton John, the New York Dolls, and the campy extravaganzas of Bette Midler and *The Rocky Horror Picture Show*." Though the troupe flopped in New York, columnist Lillian Roxon acknowledged their influence on pop culture. "Every time you see too much glitter or a rhinestone out of place, you [will] know it's because of The Cockettes," she wrote.

PART V:
Only In San Francisco

The San Francisco Bay Area is the playpen of countercultures.

– R. Z. Sheppard

Your city is remarkable not only for its beauty. It is also, of all the cities in the United States, the one whose name, the world over, conjures up the most visions and more than any other, incites one to dream.

– Georges Pompidou

The popular image of San Francisco as the cradle of the counterculture comes largely from the 1960s. No flash in the pan, the city's psychedelic era sprang from its long tradition of flamboyant rebellion. While beat poets staged their 1950s poetry renaissance in North Beach, the CIA brought LSD to town and conducted dubious mind-control experiments—drugging unwitting subjects in its covert brothel on Telegraph Hill. When local author Ken Kesey volunteered for federally funded LSD research, the drug sent him on a visionary quest.

Kesey formed the LSD-inspired Merry Pranksters, a costumed band of cultural outlaws. Hurtling cross-country in their Day-Glo schoolbus, the Pranksters hung out the windows shooting reels of film and broadcasting commentary to pedestrians. A sign on the rear read, "Caution: Weird Load." In San Francisco, the Pranksters held all-night Dionysian dance rituals called "Acid Tests" that propelled the counterculture across new frontiers of the mind.

The 1960s upheavals sprang from deep discontent with the prevailing culture. The hippies recoiled from the Vietnam war and post-war American materialism. The Free Speech Movement, across the bay in Berkeley—otherwise known as "Beserkeley"—protested university rules against political activism. In 1964, students occupied the University of California's administration building and created an alternative university—reserving the roof for sex and pot smoking—until the police handcuffed and hauled them away en masse. In 1969, Native Americans occupied Alcatraz Island, offering the U.S. $24 in glass beads and red cloth in return.

Like the Free Speech Movement, San Francisco's hippies spawned alternative institutions including the *Oracle*, a psychedelic tabloid newspaper, and the still-existing Haight-Ashbury Free Clinic. A community group called the Diggers, who gave away food and free goods, warned the hippies not to buy the media's caricatures of their movement, but to keep pushing the limits of collective transformation. "The media casts nets, creates bags for the identity hungry to climb into," the Diggers cautioned. "Your face on TV, your style immortalized without soul."

Furthering the 1960s values of participatory collective expression and radical art, Burning Man founder Larry Harvey sparked a cultural revolution when he torched an eight-foot wooden Man on San Francisco's Baker Beach. "Instead of doing art about the state of society," said Harvey, "we do art that creates society around it." The yearly Burning Man festival is constantly reinventing collective rituals for over 40,000 contemporary seekers.

San Francisco's gay communities also carried forward the 1960s' rejection of cultural conformity. In the early 1980s, the Sisters of Perpetual Indulgence—a posse of outrageous drag nuns—held the nation's first fundraisers for the AIDS crisis. Wearing rainbow-colored false eyelashes and rocket-shaped wimple headdresses, the nuns have set up sister organizations around the world and still stage bungee jumps and other fundraising stunts.

In 2004, San Francisco shook the nation when the mayor declared same-sex couples could marry. Nearly 4,000 lesbian and gay couples thronged City Hall in a loving frenzy of same-sex weddings, which the State Supreme Court later ruled illegal. As the city continues its cultural upheaval, local pundits predict it may some day secede from the Union, or break off from the continent—floating out to sea in a fabulous gesture of seismic revolt.

Jose Sarria Campaigns in Drag

Nowadays in San Francisco, it's not hard to imagine a politician campaigning for office in a gay bar, but it was unheard of in 1961 when Jose Sarria launched his bid for city supervisor at the Black Cat. At the time of his candidacy, Sarria already had a weekly gig and a large following at the bar. In various stages of drag, he performed operas—often singing all the parts and interrupting his arias with news clippings and political commentary. Each performance drew more than 300 people. At the end of the show, Sarria had the entire audience stand and sing "God Save Us Nellie Queens" to the tune of "God Save the Queen." He did not win the election, but he received a remarkable number of votes considering that his budget was less than $500, and he campaigned only during drag shows.

Though Sarria lost the election for city supervisor, he became something better. In 1965, after ongoing police harassment shut down half the city's gay bars, Sarria and a group of bar owners formed San Francisco's Tavern Guild and threw a huge public drag ball. Hundreds of drag queens arrived in limos and marched right past the cops, who parked outside the ball and took photos. During the event, Sarria proclaimed himself the Dowager Widow of the Emperor Norton, Empress of San Francisco and Protectress of Mexico, in homage to the eccentric Norton described in Part IV.

Sarria now presides over the Imperial Court of San Francisco, a fundraising institution that evolved from the Tavern Guild. The drag ball takes place annually in late February and is accompanied by the election and coronation of Empress and (drag king) Emperor.

Those seeking to establish other "royal courts" around the world must appeal to the Widow Norton and serve as a principality for two years to earn imperial status. Approximately 70 courts preside over the U.S., Mexico, Canada, England, and Germany, including the Royal Sovereign Imperial Court of All Kentucky, which raised funds for HIV/AIDS programs in the mid-1980s when no local charities would help.

Since 1965, the Dowager Widow Norton and her entourage have made yearly pilgrimages to Colma's Woodlawn cemetery to pay their respects to the Widow's departed spouse. February 2005 marked the 40th anniversary of this custom.

The Imperial Court has purchased a cemetery plot beside Norton's. The plan is that the Empress will someday be laid to rest in this spot next to her deceased husband.

Has Bert Joined Al Qaeda?

In October 2001, Reuters and the Associated Press released photographs of Bangladeshi protesters rallying against the U.S. war on Afghanistan. Some newspaper readers noticed that the demonstrators carried posters of Bert the *Sesame Street* character, side by side with Osama bin Laden. The poster images had been lifted from a San Francisco-based Web site. San Francisco artist Dino Ignacio founded the humor Web site "Bert Is Evil," where he presented doctored photographs as evidence that Ernie's friend Bert was in cahoots with Hitler and Klu Klux Klansmen.

Mostafa Kamal, production manager of the shop that made the posters, had scoured the Internet for images of bin Laden, but never noticed the stuffed toy peering over Osama's shoulder. The shop sold 2,000 posters of Osama and Bert to Bangladeshi protesters. Ignacio took down his site shortly afterward, saying, "I feel this has gotten too close to reality." Several mirror sites have kept the joke running.

The Transcendent Transamerica Pyramid

Others insist that the Bavarian Illuminati, an esoteric brotherhood related to the Freemasons, designed the Transamerica Pyramid.

The Transamerica Pyramid building at Columbus and Washington Streets is one of the few distinctive features of San Francisco's skyline. It was also one of the first buildings constructed on a set of rollers to minimize earthquake damage. But the Pyramid has sparked controversy. Some call it the "Zippy the Pinhead Building" because the architects who designed it were supposedly a bunch of stupid pinheads. Others insist that the Bavarian Illuminati, an esoteric brotherhood related to the Freemasons, designed the Transamerica Pyramid. This theory alleges that at "certain mystical moments a gigantic eye opens near the top of the building and winks at all adepts of the third degree or higher."

During an anti-war rally in 2003, demonstrators surrounded the building to protest the defense contractors who worked inside. A band of yoga practitioners called the "Underground Revolutionary Yoga Parlor" arrived during a particularly tense standoff between demonstrators and police. The yogis seemed to have a calming effect on the situation. They breathed in unison and assumed a range of challenging yoga postures as police handcuffed and hauled off the demonstrators.

Church of the Living Swing

The stand-up comedian Lord Buckley, who often appeared in public in a tuxedo, sneakers, safari hat, and a large white mustache, was among San Francisco's many early psychedelic enthusiasts. In the mid-1940s, he launched a mescaline club called the Church of the Living Swing. On a rented yacht in the San Francisco Bay, Buckley threw mescaline parties featuring live jazz by Ben Webster and Johnny Puleo and the Harmonicats.

Ferlinghetti Arrested on Obscenity Charges for Publishing *Howl*

In 1953, beat poet Lawrence Ferlinghetti and Peter D. Martin founded City Lights Bookstore. Still standing at 261 Columbus Avenue at Broadway, City Lights has provided a meeting place for writers, artists, and intellectuals for more than 50 years.

Ferlinghetti also founded City Lights Publishers, which published Allen Ginsberg's *Howl* in 1956 as part of the Pocket Poets Series. In 1957, U.S. Customs officials seized copies of *Howl*, and local authorities arrested Ferlinghetti on obscenity charges. In defense of the poem, Ferlinghetti wrote, "It is not the poet but what he observes which is revealed as obscene. The great obscene wasters of *Howl* are the sad wastes of the mechanized world, lost among atom bombs and insane nationalisms."

With the strong backing of literary and academic luminaries, Ferlinghetti was acquitted. In this landmark First Amendment case, San Francisco Superior Court Judge Clayton Horn ruled that local authorities could not censor the poem. The decision set a legal precedent for publishing controversial writing with redeeming social value. Ferlinghetti's trial turned the national media spotlight on the beat writers and the San Francisco Renaissance.

Allen Ginsberg Reads *Howl*

On October 13, 1955, six poets, Kenneth Rexroth, Allen Ginsberg, Gary Snyder, Phil Whalen, Philip Lamantia, and Michael McClure read their work at the Six Gallery on Fillmore Street. Ginsberg read his epic beat poem *Howl* for the first time.

The poem begins, "I saw the best minds of my generation destroyed by madness, starving hysterical naked, dragging themselves through the negro streets at dawn looking for an angry fix." Beat writer Jack Kerouac called the event "the night of the birth of the San Francisco poetry Renaissance." John Clellon Holmes had already coined the word "beat" in a November 1952 *New York Times* story:

> *More than mere weariness, … [beat] implies the feeling of having been used, of being raw. It involves a sort of nakedness of mind, and, ultimately, of soul: a feeling of being reduced to the bedrock of consciousness. In short, it means being undramatically pushed against the wall of oneself.*

As described in Part II, the CIA brought LSD to San Francisco in 1955 to test the drug as a weapon. After Ginsberg tried LSD courtesy of a federally funded research program, the writers and artists of San Francisco's beat movement explored psychedelics as medium for artistic and spiritual revelation.

The beats sought to subvert America's culture of conformity and map lost regions of the psyche. Allen Ginsberg described their psychedelic quests as "being part of a cosmic conspiracy… to resurrect a lost art or a lost knowledge or a lost consciousness."

In 1956, Ginsberg received a cryptic letter from his mother two days before she died. She wrote, "The key is in the window, the key is in the sunlight in the window—I have the key—get married Allen don't take drugs … Love, your mother."

Ken Kesey and the Revolt of the Guinea Pigs

Like Allen Ginsberg, author Ken Kesey first took LSD courtesy of a government research program. Kesey, a graduate student in Stanford's creative writing program, signed up for an LSD study in 1960 at the Veterans Hospital in Menlo Park, south of San Francisco.

A few weeks later, Kesey got a job as night attendant in the psychiatric ward, which housed a range of psychedelics including LSD, Ditran, mescaline, and the mysterious substance IT-290. These drugs soon made the rounds among Kesey's bohemian friends on Perry Lane. LSD also found its way into Kesey's notorious "venison chili." Kesey's acid trips and his job in the psychiatric ward sparked his widely successful first novel *One Flew Over The Cuckoo's Nest*. He dubbed the counterculture's LSD use "the revolt of the guinea pigs."

Jack Kerouac opened a million coffee bars and sold a million Levis to both sexes.

— William Burroughs

Bohemians Move from North Beach to Haight-Ashbury

In the 1940s and 1950s the folk music scene, featuring musicians such as Woody Guthrie, flourished alongside the beat movement in the coffeehouses of San Francisco's North Beach district. Comedian Lenny Bruce had his first major club engagement at Ann's 440 in January 1958. Popular hangouts included the hungry i, the Purple Onion, Vesuvio's bar, and City Lights bookstore.

But by the early 60s, tourists, organized crime, and narcotics officers strangled the North Beach hip scene. Beatniks and young bohemians fled to the Haight-Ashbury neighborhood in the working-class district called the Haight at the edge of Golden Gate Park. Haight-Ashbury became a community of cutting-edge individuals—a zone of psychedelic exploration and cultural revolt. Residents launched their own interpretation of what LSD synthesizer Albert Hoffman described as "an uninterrupted stream of fantastic pictures, extraordinary shapes with an intense, kaleidoscopic play of colors." While the old beat hipsters wore black and took a solitary approach to social alienation, the hippies wanted to form communities and raise consciousness.

By the summer of 1965, psychedelic rock and roll had taken over the folk scene in San Francisco. Every turntable played the Beatles *Rubber Soul* album. Local folkie blues and bluegrass players formed new bands such as the Warlocks (later the Grateful Dead), Country Joe and the Fish, the Charlatans, the Jefferson Airplane, and many others.

The Hippies Invent Themselves

After 20,000 attended a rally dubbed "The Human Be-In" in January 1967, reporters from news organizations around the world descended on Haight-Ashbury. *San Francisco Chronicle* columnist Herb Caen, who supposedly coined the term "beatnik," was one of the first to brand the flower children "hippies." Others claim that black musicians invented the term to dismiss the white beatnik kids slumming around the North Beach jazz scene. By the time the Blue Unicorn coffeehouse opened in 1964, the hippies had created their own culture and donned colorful clothing from hip stores such as Peggy Caserta's Mnasidika and Mike Ferguson's Magic Theater For Madmen Only—perhaps the city's first bona fide head shop. Then-California governor Ronald Reagan defined a "hippie" as someone who "dresses like Tarzan, has hair like Jane, and smells like Cheetah."

The Psychedelic Shop

Brothers Ron and Jay Thelin owned the Psychedelic Shop located near the corner of Haight and Ashbury streets. The shop, which opened in January 1966, provided a place to hang out, gossip, trade drugs, and purchase books, smoking paraphernalia, posters, and fabrics. It also started the Haight-Ashbury's first community bulletin board. Ron Thelin envisioned a time when Haight Street would become "a world famous dope center. There would be fine tea shops with big jars of fine marijuana, and chemist shops with the finest psychedelic chemicals." In a sense, Thelin's prophecy came true: Haight Street now boasts medical marijuana dispensaries that sell fine California marijuana to patients. Many other stores still sell psychedelic-themed goods.

San Francisco's Psychedelic Tabloid

During the 1960s, Haight-Ashbury had its own psychedelic tabloid newspaper, the *San Francisco Oracle*—a beacon for the counterculture in San Francisco and around the world. Allen Cohen, who worked part time at the Psychedelic Shop had a vision of a "rainbow colored newspaper." Ron Thelin gave him $500 to make his dream real, and in September 1966, Cohen launched the *San Francisco Oracle*.

The *Oracle* published stories about eastern mysticism, astrology, macrobiotics, yoga, and other topics that few contemporary newspapers covered. When the

California Legislature outlawed the use of LSD on October 6, 1966, the *Oracle* pointed out that the Bible claimed "666" as the mark of the Beast or the devil. On a more serious note, the paper said the edict violated people's right to explore religious transcendence. "We were not guilty of using illegal substances," said founder Allen Cohen. "We were celebrating transcendental consciousness, the beauty of the universe, the beauty of being."

The *Oracle* folded in February 1968, when the Haight-Ashbury district came under intense scrutiny by national and local authorities.

International Hippie Magnet

In 1966, kids from all over the world flooded Haight-Ashbury to participate in the Dionysiac revelry that drew long-hairs with different values from mainstream America. In the first six months of 1966, San Francisco reportedly harbored 1,231 runaways. An estimated 15,000 hippies lived in Haight-Ashbury. Many formed collective households. The community met and posted messages at the Psychedelic Shop at 1535 Haight Street. They read the newly launched *San Francisco Oracle* newspaper and lined up for health care at the Haight-Ashbury Free Clinic. Young people from all over the world still come to Haight Street seeking that ethereal community vibe.

Bigfoot Museum

The search for Bigfoot (or the sasquatch) has been going on for hundreds of years in the hills of northern California—San Francisco celebrated the hunt for this mythical creature by opening a museum dedicated to the beast. Billed as the city's "strangest museum," the North Beach archive was opened in 1997 by local eccentric Eric Beckjord and was devoted to the study of Bigfoot, as well as other phenomena such as the Loch Ness Monster and UFOs.

Beckjord claimed to be totally serious about his collection, which consisted mainly of photographs, drawings, and articles tacked to the wall, such as the Roswell Declaration and supposed real-life images of Bigfoot. The back wall was devoted to Sassie, a sea serpent rumored to live in San Francisco Bay.

The museum is currently closed, but San Francisco's legion of Bigfoot fans need not despair. There is now a bar on Polk Street devoted to the beast with a statue—captured in resin and standing at a towering height of nine feet, six inches—with log cabin decor and Bigfoot memorabilia on the walls. In the interests of safety, patrons are recommended not to go out looking for their idol after a night out at The Bigfoot Lodge.

The North Beach archive was opened in 1997 by a local eccentric.

Manson Seeks Stardom

Many of the flower children came to San Francisco seeking spiritual transcendence. This quest made them vulnerable to power trippers, hustlers and rip off artists who preyed on their desire to shed the self and merge with cosmic consciousness. The Haight-Ashbury Research Project estimated that 15 percent of the people who flocked to the Haight were "psychotic fringe and religious obsessives."

Charles Manson camped out on the Straight Theater's roof and recruited a number of his "Manson Family" followers from the Haight. While in San Francisco, Manson wrote his best-known song, "The Ego Is A Too Much Thing." Seeking stardom, he moved his cult from Haight-Ashbury to Los Angeles, but the music industry rejected his work. Manson was only one of many "psychic vampires" who preyed on people in Haight-Ashbury.

Summer of Love

The so-called Summer of Love saw dark clouds gathering over Haight-Ashbury. Toward mid-summer 1967, the police cracked down on marijuana and acid dealers in the neighbourhood. Crystal methedrine and heroin flooded the streets and created a menacing, paranoid atmosphere. Speed ravaged the district—causing sickness, appetite suppression, and consequent malnutrition. Many people shot speed and heroin. Years later they learned they had contracted hepatitis C by sharing needles. The Haight-Ashbury Free Clinic opened to address the public health crisis.

Police launched a major drug bust at the Grateful Dead's house at 710 Ashbury, and pictures of their post-arrest gig appeared in the first issue of *Rolling Stone*. During the raid, the cops managed to miss an entire kilo of grass in full view in the pantry.

This tumultuous time also saw the murders of several local drug sellers, including John Kent "Shob" Carter. The killer cut Carter's hand off his corpse, probably because he had handcuffed his money briefcase to it. In September 1967, San Francisco's Straight Theater screened Kenneth Anger's film *Lucifer Rising* with a soundtrack by Manson Family member "Bummer" Bobby Beausoleil and his Chamber Orkustra. In October, the Diggers organized a "Death of the Hippie" march on Haight Street. At the end of the march, protestors stopped outside the Psychedelic Shop and buried the store's sign.

Tensions also escalated between white hippies and black residents of the nearby Fillmore district. Community leaders such as poet Gary Snyder suggested that hippies "tribalize," form self-sustaining communes, and move to the country. Many did just that. By 1968, the Broadway musical *Hair* had commercially repackaged the hippie scene.

Holding Out for a Hero

San Francisco mayor Frank Jordan was keen to honor a true hero—if only he knew who it was. During an apartment fire, a frantic mother tossed her three children from her third-story window into the arms of a passerby. The mother and all of the children survived. When a press release later went out asking the passerby to identify himself to receive his honors, four men stepped forward to say it was them who had caught the children.

Strange Stand-off

In January 2004, police were called to South Beach Marina to investigate a bizarre hostage taking. A woman called them and reported that she had been taken captive for the past two days by a group of four people, armed with guns and explosives. It was reported that the group had taken over her apartment on Townsend Street on Monday, but allowed her to go to work on Wednesday, where she telephoned the police. When the police raided the apartment after a two-hour standoff, they discovered a number of BB guns, smoke grenades, and a replica Uzi. Although the woman knew one of her attackers, no motive was given for the hostage taking.

The group had taken over her apartment on Townsend Street.

On the Farm

The Farm, a large commune in Tennessee, began as a college course at San Francisco State University in the mid 1960s. "Monday Night Class," as it was called, moved into a concert hall called the Family Dog and up to 1,500 people attended each week. In 1969, Gaskin left San Francisco to go on a speaking tour of liberal churches across the United States, taking many members of his class along with him. The motley caravan eventually included 400 hippies, traveling in 50 school buses and 40 other vehicles. After 7,000 miles and seven months, the caravan came back to San Francisco. Instead of splitting up, they decided to return to Tennessee and find a place where they could all live communally. At its peak in the 1970s, 2,000 people lived on the Farm and 10,000 visited each year.

Bring On the Marching Band

The Extra Action Marching Band is about as far from the traditional marching band as you can get. A troupe of around 30 musicians, with full drum and horn sections, they are more likely to play twisted funk than standard show tunes and prefer unannounced performances to established gigs. Formed in early 1998, the band frequently gatecrash events such as celebrity book signings, record stores, and even private homes to put on their unusual live shows. The band also has a flag team who tend to attract the most attention with their gender-bending outfits and sexual dance moves. In 2000, when they were booked to play a piercers' convention in Las Vegas, the team stripped down to beaded g-strings while standing atop the slot machines. Attracting many new members over the years, the group has recently had to add a pep squad to accommodate the extra band mates. They are planning to put out a CD of their live show and hope to continue spreading anarchy for many years to come.

Car Thief Demands Compensation

A man was convicted of stealing a San Francisco Bay Area couple's car at gunpoint. The thief then filed suit from prison, demanding $2,794 compensation for the loss of personal property that he left in the car he stole. Police gave the items, mostly clothing, to charity, before returning the car to its owners.

Death at Altamont

In December 1969, the Rolling Stones concluded their American tour at Altamont Speedway stadium in Livermore, east of San Francisco. Owsley, the acid chemist, said Altamont "was like a moonscape of crushed auto bodies, it looked like a skull and I thought, 'this place smells of death.' " The Stones hired the Hell's Angels to provide security at the concert, but unknowingly brought together rival factions locked in an escalating gang war. The bikers thrashed innocent concertgoers and stabbed spectator Meredith Hunter to death a few feet from Mick Jagger. Many saw Altamont as a curtain call for the decade.

LSD and Beyond

During the Golden Age of Haight-Ashbury, many people embraced LSD as a catalyst for a new form of culture. As the 1960s came to a close, some followed Timothy Leary, who saw LSD as a doorway to a Garden of Eden, which blurred distinctions between matter and spirit. Leary preached the death of the ego and the rebirth of consciousness. But the trip was rockier for some than for others. Many people simply wondered, what came next? Ken Kesey and other leaders of the San Francisco psychedelic scene advised tripsters to "graduate" from the acid experience and find non-chemical ways to expand consciousness, form communities, agitate for political change, and attune themselves to the world around them.

The psychedelic movement in San Francisco sparked new cultural movements around the world—including women's rights, environmentalism, organic foods, alternative sexual expression, meditation, and yoga. San Francisco remains a center of the current yoga craze sweeping the world.

Indians Occupy Alcatraz

On March 9, 1964, five Sioux Indians occupied the abandoned federal prison on Alcatraz Island in the San Francisco Bay. Citing an 1868 treaty that the United

States made with the Sioux, occupiers claimed that the abandoned facility had reverted back to Indian land. The occupation lasted only four hours, but on November 9, 1969, a group of 78 Native American college students called "Indians of All Tribes" returned to Alcatraz for 19 months.

Led by Richard Oakes and Adam Fortunate Eagle, the group claimed the island for an Indian university, museum, and cultural center. They issued a proclamation offering to pay the federal government "24 dollars ($24) in glass beads and red cloth"—the sum that the Dutch paid for Manhattan Island in 1626, according to popular legend.

The island remained Indian land until June 10, 1971, when 20 armed marshals, special forces police, and FBI agents removed the 15 unarmed residents, composed of five women, six men, and four children. Though the occupation ended, it drew worldwide attention to the Native American demand for self-determination.

The Sisters of Perpetual Indulgence

If you've gone to San Francisco's Pink Saturday (the night before the city's Bisexual, Lesbian, Gay, and Transgender Pride Parade), chances are you've dropped a few dollars in the bucket of a six-foot-tall nun wearing a white face, rainbow-colored false eyelashes, and a rocket-shaped wimple headdress, known as "ear brassieres."

Your cash went to an excellent cause. The Sisters of Perpetual Indulgence—a 100 percent volunteer non-profit organization—have raised more than one million dollars for non-profits serving gay communities and other worthy causes in the last 24 years.

The Sisters take their role as nuns very seriously. As they say on their Web site (www.thesisters.org):

We are very dedicated to our calling and our vows reflect our commitment to our community…We minister to our flock…We raise funds for the needy…We are educators…The list goes on and on … and yes, we spank too.

Rather than taking a vow of chastity, each fully professed nun vows "to promulgate universal joy and to expiate stigmatic guilt."

The Sisters trace their origins to the day before Easter 1979, when four gay men took to the streets in full nuns' habits. By 1980, they had ordained more nuns, named themselves the Sisters of Perpetual Indulgence, and chosen individual names such as Sister Ahhanarisvara, Sister Missionary Position, and Sister Roz Erection. Sister Hysterectoria designed their customary habits and wimple, modeled on the headdress of 14th-century Flemish ladies-in-waiting.

The Sisters of Perpetual Indulgence have been at the forefront of AIDS activism since 1982 when Sister Florence Nightmare and Sister Roz Erection, both registered nurses, contributed to "Play Fair," the first widely circulated safer sex pamphlet. That same year the Sisters organized the first AIDS fundraiser, a dog show on Castro Street emceed by Shirley MacLaine. Sister Boom Boom also ran for Supervisor on the "Nun of the Above" ticket. She gleaned 23,000 votes.

While the original Sisters were gay men in San Francisco, the group now embraces all genders and orientations. Sister organizations have spread to Australia, Colombia, England, France, Germany, Scotland, Los Angeles, Seattle, and the Midwest.

When Pope John Paul II visited San Francisco in 1987, the Sisters welcomed him with a red carpet and performed an exorcism in Union Square. Some claim that this earned the Sisters a place on the Papal List of Heretics, though others say this is an urban myth.

Many San Francisco residents fondly remember the day that several Sisters bungee-jumped from the top of a crane in a downtown San Francisco park. The Sisters also hold a popular "Hunky Jesus" contest in Dolores Park each Easter Sunday. During last year's event, one of the competitors later ran as a candidate for the local school board. He was hunky, but he did not win. Only in San Francisco can you find an electoral candidate participating in a Hunky Jesus contest run by drag nuns.

A San Franciscan Life

Antonio Bettencourt is a fifth-generation San Franciscan, interviewed for this book, who has seen many changes in the city over the years. In 1969, when Antonio was eight-years-old and living on Coleridge Street in Bernal Heights, a man played loud rock music with other musicians every day in a nearby empty lot surrounded by a broken chain link fence. This drove Antonio's mother to the edge of her wits. She hated rock music and would run down the street banging pots and pans, screaming at this crazy man to stop making his infernal noise. As it turned out, this annoying neighbor was the now-famous rock musician Carlos Santana.

There was a bank in Berkeley that Antonio used to go to with his mother. One day in 1972, they went to the bank, and the building was gone. It had been blown up by the Symbionese Liberation Army, Patty Hearst's kidnappers.

Mad Scientists

Survival Research Laboratories (SRL) is a group of Bay Area technicians who create machine art—their goal is to radically redirect scientific and technological concepts away from industrial and military applications. Performing worldwide, the group stages mechanized spectacles featuring ritual interactions between machines, robots, and devices that produce fiery special effects. Many SRL events satirize contemporary politics and culture. They also relegate humans to the margins of the machine world—as audience members or machine operators.

Founded by Mark Pauline in November 1978, SRL has created a number of memorable machines, including the "Flame Hurricane," a 5,000-pound instrument that uses Pulse Jet engines to produce "a rapidly rotating column of hot, high velocity hurricane-like fire." The "Pitching Machine" launches two-by-four boards at 250 mph. The "Hand-O'-God" is "a giant spring loaded hand cocked by a hydraulic cylinder with 8 tons of pressure." The "Flame Whistle" is the loudest flamethrower in history. Some of these machines make appearances at street parties in and around San Francisco. Crowds marvel at the action.

An Odd Treasure Hunt

Each year, San Francisco residents gather for an unusual sleuthing adventure that takes place during the chaos of the Chinese New Year celebration. As dragons parade through the streets and firecrackers fill the air, teams assemble to compete in the Chinese New Year Treasure Hunt, played out on the

As dragons parade through the streets and firecrackers fill the air, teams assemble to compete in the treasure hunt.

streets of Chinatown, North Beach, and Telegraph Hill. The teams have four hours to solve 16 clues. Each clue leads them to some forgotten landmark, obscure architectural feature, or piece of San Francisco history. The teams must find each location and record some detail or answer a riddle to prove that they have arrived in the right place. Participants often discover new nuggets of San Francisco history, such as the alley where Sam Spade's partner was gunned down in *The Maltese Falcon*.

Suicide Club Sewer Tours

In the 1970s, the San Francisco Suicide Club carried on the beat generation's tradition of collective urban adventuring. A former club member recalls the days when you could mail the club $5 and a stack of envelopes: They would send back a newsletter listing the strange events that the club sponsored. The mysterious event listings often required members to bring flashlights, gas up their cars, and wear dark clothing. Participants called a special telephone number to find out the location of the event and ENTER THE UNKNOWN.

Events included formal dress tours of the Oakland storm sewers featuring groups of 40 to 50 people in hip boots and eveningwear. On one occasion, the group ventured into a rerouted sewer and ran into a concrete wall. Participants climbed up to street level and waited in a small vacant lot surrounded by chain link fence, while other members of the group scouted ahead for an available route. A barking dog prompted neighbors to call the police. When the officers arrived, organizers explained that the group was headed to Mills College for a potluck supper. The two officers looked at the group's fancy dress, glanced at each other, shrugged and said, "Only in Oakland."

Some Suicide Club members also enjoyed a team game known as Inter-Hotelic Star Wars. Teams armed themselves with different colors of glitter. Dressed as businesspeople, they circulated through the lobbies and public spaces of four different hotels. The goal was to sprinkle glitter on the leader of the opposing team. Since each team kept its leader's identity secret from the other, any member of the opposing team was a potential target. Participants took care to avoid detection. Hotel detectives caught the players only once.

World's Oldest Snackreligion

The First Church of the Last Laugh is the world's oldest "snackreligion." One of the main benefits of this church is that it has only one holiday: April Fools' Day. Each year on April 1, the St. Stupid's Day Parade marches through downtown San Francisco and the financial district. They throw pennies at the lumpish stone statue called "The Bankers Heart," located in front of the Bank of America building.

Marchers wear stupid costumes, carry stupid signs, engage in stupid conversations, and celebrate stupidity in all its forms. The parade ends at the San

Francisco Stock Exchange, where the participants exchange socks. They treasure the sayings of St. Stupid, such as, "We have nothing to fear, but fear ourselves."

More Suicide Club Adventures

The Suicide Club pioneered many urban adventures that later developed into San Francisco traditions. They have hosted elaborate urban treasure hunts in which players searched for clues in the ruins of the old Sutro Baths or in various World War II era concrete bunkers built into the seaside cliffs surrounding the city. When players solved the last clue in the treasure hunt and arrived at the destination, they would often find a cache of cream pies that they were supposed to hurl at members of opposing teams. These treasure hunts helped give rise to the annual Chinese New Year Treasure Hunt.

During one memorable event known as "Let Them Eat Cake," Suicide Club members made a statement about social inequality by dressing as 18th-century French aristocrats and serving cake on the local BART subway trains.

The Billboard Liberation Front

In September 1977, 26 urban adventurers attended an evening where they were blindfolded, driven to an inner city freeway exchange, and "cajoled into climbing onto a factory roof where they improved two existing billboard messages." After alterations, the former cosmetics ad read, "Warning! A Pretty Face Isn't Safe

in This City. Fight Back With Self-Abuse. The New Mutilator Ax Factor."
The perpetrators became known as the "Max Factor 26" after authorities
caught them.

Two members of the Max Factor 26, Jack Napier and Irving Glikk, formed
the Billboard Liberation Front (BLF), which altered outdoor advertisements.
According to the group's philosophy, billboard changes had to be "factually
accurate and easy to remove." In the wee hours of the morning, the BLF
prowled the streets of San Francisco—searching for billboards that needed
"improvement." Before BLF, a billboard for Fact cigarettes read, "I'm realistic. I
only smoke Facts." After BLF, the ad read, "I'm real sick. I only smoke Facts." A
large arrow pointed to the surgeon general's warning on the billboard. An ad for
Camel cigarettes featured a swarthy bare-chested man—until the liberators
adorned him with a pink brassiere.

The BLF eventually chose official spokespeople, issued press releases, and
claimed 350 conspirators. Billboard liberators stage elaborate rehearsals and
deploy extensive ground crews to warn of impending interference during the
operations. Alterations range from simple to complex and from subtle to
the not so subtle. The popular "dot-com" campaign involved 10 dot-com
company billboards along the 101 freeway "Silicon Valley" corridor. The BLF
enhanced these ads with the phrase: "FATAL ERROR—Invalid Stock Value
Abort/Retry/Fail."

The BLF completed its most recent work in June 2004. The billboard called for California Governor and Terminator cyborg Arnold Schwarzenegger to fight "killer robots." It reads: "Arnold: 1,300,000 cyborgs in California in 2002 alone…HELP!," signed by "Citizens Against Killer Robots. N. Cal. 1 800 215 2352." BLF founder Jack Napier says, "We recognize that this issue places Governor Schwarzenegger in an awkward position, being a cyborg himself."

The San Francisco Cacophony Society

The successor to the San Francisco Suicide Club, or perhaps its weird younger brother, is the San Francisco Cacophony Society. On their Web site, the group describes itself as "a randomly gathered network of free spirits united in pursuit of experiences beyond the pale of mainstream society… We are the Merry Pranksters of a new decade." The society further defines itself as "nonpolitical, nonprophet, and often nonsensical."

Like its predecessor the Suicide Club, members gather for participatory experiences, such as the St. Stupid's Day Parade. On January 8, the Cacophony Society commemorates Emperor Norton's Death with a visit to his Colma gravesite. On April 19, members observe "Reflection Day for government employees."

The Cacophony Society puts out a monthly newsletter and calendar of events. Festivities include the annual Santa Rampage, where a group of drunken, crabby revelers dress in cheap Santa suits and roam the streets of San Francisco abusing bystanders. One year, the Santas ran amuck through Macy's department store chanting, "Charge it!"

"The Cacophony Society has no leaders, no organization, and no rules," reads their site. "You may already be a member!"

Bridge Climbing

The towers of the Golden Gate and Bay Bridges reach more than 500 feet above the bay. Outfitting themselves with gloves, sweatshirts, chocolate truffles, and champagne, adventurers climb at night to avoid being seen. One Halloween, they hoisted a carved jack-o-lantern up the towers.

The west tower of the Bay Bridge stands at the end of a pier on the San Francisco waterfront. One reaches it by scaling a fence on a nearby pier and navigating nearby docks and catwalks. At the base of the bridge tower, one leaps over a bit of barbed wire fence to reach maintenance ladders located inside the two giant metal X's that support the towers. The towers' doors are unlocked at each level. It takes at least an hour to climb up a series of 12-foot enclosed cells inside the tower, but from the observation deck, one has a superb view of the city, 525 feet above the bay.

The Golden Gate Bridge also has an observation deck, which one reaches by climbing the cells inside the towers. Unlike the Bay Bridge, the Golden Gate has an elevator. Most secret bridge climbers avoid it for fear of making noise or attracting attention. From the observation deck, one can stand directly on the cables that support the bridge. The cables are about as wide as a sidewalk. On either side the bridge has guy wires one can use as railings.

One climber took his hands off the wires just to see how it felt. He quickly grabbed them again, as the wind almost swept him off the cable. One night, he and his friends watched silently as a car stopped on the bridge. The driver wandered out, only to be apprehended by police. "Our goal was not to draw attention to ourselves," the climber said, "but just to be there and have an adventure and explore the city and then leave no trace or indication that we had been there." Since sharpshooters now guard San Francisco's bridges against terrorist attacks, one must take extra care to avoid being seen.

Chicago is the great American city, New York is one of the capitals of the world, and Los Angeles is a constellation of plastic; San Francisco is a lady.

— Norman Mailer

Burning Man

Burning Man, a ritualistic yearly arts festival, takes place on the Black Rock Desert, north of Reno, Nevada. The event began in 1986 with a spontaneous act of renewal on San Francisco's Baker Beach. Burning Man Founder Larry Harvey was suffering heartbreak after parting from a girlfriend. The two had attended annual summer solstice celebrations at Baker Beach. As another solstice approached, Harvey anticipated that he would miss his ex at this year's event.

During one solstice, a friend had set fire to three mannequins in leisure suits strapped into a car seat. On a whim, Harvey, then a landscape gardener, decided to build an eight-foot wooden Man, douse it with gasoline, and torch it on the beach during the solstice. As the sculpture burned, a woman ran up to the pyre and held the Man's hand, as the wind blew the flames aside. A musician played a song, and the entire group sang along.

Transfixed by the event, Harvey pursued his longstanding interest in ritual and sacred architecture. He continued to burn the Man on the summer solstice—by the fourth year, the Man had grown to four stories in height and the event had outgrown Baker Beach. Harvey and friends moved the burn to the Black Rock Desert. As time passed, Harvey became more interested in people's response to the ritual than in the flaming figure itself. In 1993, the event drew 1,000 participants. Three years later it expanded to 10,000 rugged souls willing to brave the harsh desert environment.

Burning Man has now grown into a 10-day gathering of 40,000-plus people. During the festival, participants build an entire metropolis called Black Rock City. At the festival's close, they dismantle the city—returning the playa (or desert) to a pristine state. Though people buy tickets to the event, Black Rock City is removed from the world of corporate sponsorship and prohibits vending, aside from a stand that sells ice and a central café that sells beverages. In place of monetary transactions, Burning Man encourages a "gift economy." People give services and art projects to strangers and to the community without requiring something in return. Instead of bringing only what they need to survive, participants construct elaborate "theme camps," including matchmaking services, hair-washing stations, massage camps, free grilled fish stands, and "slow-dance pavilions."

The Man Who Flogs Cars

On a hot summer's day in 1989, two young women inadvertently swerved in front of a man driving a convertible on Market Street. At the next stoplight, the man, wearing a seersucker suit and a patch over one eye, pulled up behind them, leaped out of his car, removed a bullwhip from his trunk, and got back in his car. When the light changed, the man trailed the women down Market Street and through the Mission, flogging the back of their car with his bullwhip. The chase took place on heavily trafficked streets in broad daylight, but no one seemed to notice. It was just another day in San Francisco. Finally, when the women pulled up in front of a police station on Valencia Street, the man drove off and left them alone.

Same-Sex Weddings

In February 2004, San Francisco mayor Gavin Newsom announced that same-sex couples should have the opportunity to marry. From February 12, until a court order halted the ceremonies on March 11, 3,955 lesbian and gay couples rushed to the altar in a mass outpouring of same-sex union. Six months later, the State Supreme Court ruled that Newsom had defied the law defining marriage as the union of a man and a woman. Stating that the same-sex newlyweds were not legally married or entitled to the rights of spouses, the court ordered the city to refund each couple their $82 license fee and the $62 fee for the wedding ceremony.

> *Lesbian and gay couples rushed to the altar in a mass outpouring of same-sex union.*

San Francisco—A Favorite Haunt for Ghosts

San Francisco boasts an unusually high incidence of ghost sightings—though "ghost sightings" are hard to quantify, since many people do not believe in spirits. Some who do believe say that the dead never forgave the city for evicting them. In the early twentieth century, the Board of Supervisors exiled all graveyards to

Colma, south of San Francisco. In some cases, the city saved time and money by moving headstones to Colma and leaving the interments underground.

Jim Fassbinder, who "began seeing ghosts as a small boy," leads the San Francisco Ghost Hunt, a two-hour tour of the city's ghostly sites. He attributes the high number of hauntings to the city's "wild and wicked history … A ghost is an extreme emotion stuck in time," says Fassbinder. "You put money, sin, earthquakes, fire, greed, saloons, everything together—you've got a lot of emotion."

Antoinette May, the author of *Haunted Houses of California*, agrees with Fassbinder. "Places where people live very full and colorful lives seem to attract a lot of energy," she says. "People just don't want to be dead—they want to come back and raise hell."

Frustrated Artists Haunt Art Institute

The San Francisco Art Institute at 800 Chesnut Street stands on the former site of a cemetery. Since the Institute opened in January 1927, numerous students and professors have reported footsteps climbing the stairs of the bell tower, lights switching on and off, doors opening and closing, and other poltergeist-like activity. Wally Hendrick, a longtime faculty member, claimed that one night all the power tools in the sculpture studio simultaneously turned on by themselves. Art Institute denizens believed the ghost was harmless until 1968, when a string of near-deadly and expensive mishaps delayed the renovation of the bell tower for months.

When psychics held a séance in the bell tower, one San Jose medium, Amy Chandler, saw a "lost graveyard." Others blamed frustrated ambitions—"so many artists with such grand designs that never got anywhere." Ghost photographer Nick Nocerino took a series of photos that showed the inside of the tower as it once looked, with windows and a door that were no longer there at the time of the séance.

Atherton House

In 1881, Chilean-born Dominga de Goni Atherton built a mansion that still stands on the corner of California and Octavia. Dominga's son George Atherton married Gertrude, a feminist who penned racy romance novels and called her husband a "mere male, nothing more." In 1887, Gertrude threw a ball at the Atherton House to honor some Chilean naval officers visiting the city. The ladies in traditional ball gowns with bustles and voluminous tulle were scandalized when Gertrude appeared in a slinky white cashmere thing "fitting every part of me like a glove."

Weary of his wife's contempt, George jumped at an invitation to accompany the naval officers back to Chile. But he died of kidney failure after only a few days at sea. The Chileans shipped George home to San Francisco for burial.

Hoping to preserve the body, they stuffed it inside a barrel of rum. The Athertons learned of George's death only after the barrel arrived on their doorstep at 1990 California Street. The butler opened the crate and discovered his pickled employer inside. Gertrude claimed her inheritance and ran from the house, saying, "I had an uneasy feeling George would haunt me if he could."

In 1923, an odd cat-lover named Carrie Rousseau remodeled the Atherton House—dividing the mansion at 1990 California Street into separate apartments. Rousseau chose the 13th unit—the grand ballroom's orchestra chamber—for herself and moved her cats into the adjoining banquet hall. They remained until 1974, when Rousseau died, a 93-year-old recluse, attended by more than 50 feline friends.

After numerous ghost sightings at the Atherton House, ghost researcher Antoinette May and psychic Sylvia Brown held a séance onsite. "Hot and cold running spirits made the evening memorable," writes May. "Room temperatures changed frequently and drastically, keeping the 11 of us who participated in the séance busy putting on and taking off our jackets and sweaters." Ghostchaser Nick Nocerino took photographs, which showed a number of glowing "blobs" floating around the house.

"There is a male spirit here," said Brown, "but he's so pale and frail. There's nothing to fear from him. But bad vibes could come from the female spirits who want things done their way." The psychic identified a short, buxom, and volatile ghost, who kept insisting, "This is my dwelling," as well as an attractive blond apparition who was "very independent for her time."

Those familiar with the house's history recognized the male spirit as George Atherton, the short, buxom ghost as Dominga de Goni Atherton, and the blond as Gertrude. A fourth ghost—the eccentric cat-lover Carrie Rousseau—also haunted the mansion. Since the female spirits clearly wore the pants in this mansion, the psychic said the Atherton House would make a great women's resource center.

Current tenants at 1990 California Street hear murmurs and whispers under the staircase—where the Athertons stored the barrel of rum containing George's corpse. "Just about every resident reports seeing a glowing ball of light in their room on the first night staying at the house," writes Heather Knight, reporting for the *San Francisco Chronicle*.

One tenant, Alden Cady, didn't believe in ghosts when he first moved into his wife's apartment. But on the first night, as he lay in bed trying to fall asleep, he noticed a mysterious glow. "I'm kind of a logical, scientific guy, so I was really trying to figure out where this glow was coming from," says Cady. "I turned on the lights. I turned off the lights. I opened the shades. I closed the shades. I couldn't affect it at all. It was pretty wild. I didn't know if I was going nuts."

When he told his wife, Tracy, and other residents about the glow, they said it was Gertrude Atherton, the feminist romance writer. One night, Cady and Tracy had a "whopper of a fight" and went to bed without apologizing. As Cady lay in bed steaming, his car horn began blaring in the street below.

He dashed downstairs, pulled fuses, and banged on the steering wheel, but nothing worked. "All of a sudden, I thought of Gertrude and I said, 'OK, Gertrude, I'll go up and apologize to Tracy,' and the horn stopped," says Cady. "That was spooky. I went upstairs, and I apologized and everything was OK from then on."

While female residents tend to stay in the apartment complex for years, most men who move in leave within a few months says Cady, who now believes in ghosts. Brown says the strong-willed female ghosts "won't tolerate much male interference."

New Orleans is one of the two most ingrown, self-obsessed little cities in the United States. The other is San Francisco.

— Nora Ephron

Sally Stanford—Bootlegger, Madam, Mayor

In 1976, Sally Stanford, San Francisco's most notorious madam, became the mayor of Sausalito, the sleepy town just north of the Golden Gate Bridge. Stanford is perhaps the only elected official in U.S. history who succeeded in politics after a long, distinguished career running brothels.

Born Mabel Janice Busby in 1903, Stanford opened her first bordello in the early 1930s—supposedly after the police raided a hotel she owned on O'Farrell Street. As Stanford had recently divorced a lawyer, the morning headline announced, "Wife of Prominent Attorney Arrested for Running a Disorderly House." Stanford swore she was innocent of the charges, but the false claim propelled her into the business as she figured she might as well capitalize on her reputation.

Stanford's business flourished during World War II, when troops passed through the city on their way to the war in the Pacific. When the United Nations drew up their charter in San Francisco in 1945, Stanford said, "We had so many ambassadors in the place that if we had been raided, I could have declared diplomatic immunity."

Stanford's most famous establishment was the "Fortress" at 1144 Pine Street, several blocks from the swank downtown hotels. *San Francisco Chronicle* columnist Herb Caen called it "The Sally Stanford School for Advanced Social Studies." *Life* magazine ran a story on Stanford saying that "Miss Stanford and her specially selected hostesses entertained princes and shahs, movie stars, state and national dignitaries; some of her customers even brought their wives."

For years the vice squad failed to infiltrate the Fortress. To enter, one had to pass an iron gate, an outdoor waiting area, then a heavy door leading to a winding staircase. Sergeant John Dyer and other vice cops posed as clients—

donning fake mustaches and dinner jackets—but nothing worked. Stanford said the "secretaries" were busy and recommended another "dictating service" nearby. Once, Stanford saw Dyer peering in through the skylight. She phoned the police, reported a peeping Tom, and watched the cops show up and arrest the plainclothes officer. At his disability hearing, Dyer claimed his efforts to "nail Sally Stanford" had contributed to his heart condition.

When the police finally breached the Fortress in 1949, they found only a rumpled bed, two half-empty drinks, and two cigarettes still burning in an ashtray. They combed the building, but couldn't find where everyone had gone. The police seized files, but when District Attorney Edmund "Pat" Brown opened Stanford's book of clients and saw lists of politicians, celebrities, dignitaries, and world leaders, he refused to release the names as it could potentially have jeopardized his career.

After the raid, Stanford retired and moved to Sausalito, where she became a successful restaurateur, a city council member, and eventually mayor. Her memoirs were made into a movie, *The Lady of the House* (1978), and she achieved such high social standing that, when she married into the prominent Gump family, columnist Herb Caen overheard the following conversation in Gump's store: "You say the Gump family is important here?" a tourist asked. Another replied, "Oh, quite. Why, one of them recently married into the Stanford clan."

Dear Jesse

Each year the San Francisco International Lesbian and Gay Film Festival asks audience members to vote on their favorite films and presents awards based on their response. In 1998, San Francisco audiences chose Tim Kirkman's *Dear Jesse* as Best Documentary. In this film, Kirkman, a gay filmmaker, returns to his hometown in North Carolina, the political stomping ground of ultra-conservative anti-gay Senator Jesse Helms, who is something of a pariah in left-leaning San Francisco. Festival producers write, "Kirkman and Helms have a few qualities in common: they were born within three miles of one another, they attended the same college, and they are 'both obsessed with gay men.'"

City Tears Down Literary Landmark

In 1959, San Francisco tore down the Montgomery Block—the most illustrious literary landmark in the American West—and built a parking lot. While this may surprise tourists, residents know how hard it is to find parking.

The four-story Montgomery Block, built in 1853, housed literary greats such as Ambrose Bierce, Gelett Burgess, Joaquin Miller, W. C. Morrow, Kathleen Norris, George Sterling, James Hopper, and thousands of other writers and artists. In the Montgomery Block steam baths, Mark Twain met San Francisco fireman Tom Sawyer, whose name Twain later made famous. Dr. Sun Yat-sen—later hailed as "Father of the Chinese Revolution"—stayed in the Montgomery Block during his exile and penned a new Chinese constitution, which he installed when the Manchu dynasty collapsed in 1911.

The Transamerica Pyramid building at 600 Montgomery Street now stands on the former site of the Montgomery Block.

The "Spite Fence"

San Francisco self-made tycoon Charles Crocker would stop at nothing to get his way. While managing the construction of the Central Pacific Railroad, Crocker overcame labor shortages by importing Chinese workers, who took on dangerous, backbreaking tasks at very low pay. The completion of the Central Pacific in 1869 made Crocker one of the richest men in the nation. He joined the ranks of San Francisco's other land barons by building himself a palace on Nob Hill.

For the site of his mansion, Crocker chose the block between California, Jones, Sacramento, and Taylor Streets. A dozen houses stood on this block, but most of the homeowners were willing to sell. Only one, a Chinese undertaker named Nicholas Yung, refused to move. When Crocker offered a generous $3,000, Yung requested $6,000. When Crocker agreed, Yung asked for $12,000, then $40,000. Furious, Crocker called off negotiations and told his architects to design his house around Yung's 40-by-100 foot lot.

By 1877, Crocker had a mansion that rivaled Nob Hill's other gaudy castles. His critics dubbed it "nightmare wedding cake" and "delirium of the wood carver." Crocker approached Yung one last time. When the undertaker still refused, Crocker was so mad he built a 40-foot-tall fence around Yung's entire property, so he'd never have to see him again. When the fence was finished, Yung, who had previously had a view of the Golden Gate and the Bay, could now not see daylight. Newspapers from around the world ran stories on the "spite fence." Tourists came to gawk at it.

Meanwhile, Crocker's importation of cheap Chinese labor had awakened fierce racial tensions. By the mid-1870s, the Asian railroad workers had formed the nation's largest Chinatown in San Francisco. Dennis Kearney, a fiery spokesman for the extremist socialist Workingman's party, delivered racist harangues against the Chinese. Because they worked long hours under appalling conditions for intolerably low wages, he accused them of trying to steal white men's jobs. But Kearney harbored an even greater hatred for Crocker's greed and abuse of workers.

On October 29, 1877, Kearney led an angry mob of 3,000 up Nob Hill to Crocker's mansion and commanded them to tear down the spite fence. "This is the symbol," shouted Kearney. "This is the way the overlords crush the little men." The mob charged the 40-foot wall and hurled their bodies against it. Yung crouched inside, terrified that the fence would fall and crush his house, but the wall wouldn't budge.

Several months later, Yung sold the land baron his property for $6,000 and moved into a larger, safer abode. Crocker installed a rack of rifles by his front door and swore he'd shoot Kearney if he ever showed up again. Kearney never did. A few years after his assault on the wall, his rich uncle died and left him a fortune. Kearney abandoned labor politics and built his own mansion. Occasionally, he stopped by Crocker's office and asked him to recount the story of how he tried to knock down the fence. The two men would compare notes and laugh.

Ghost Cop Writes Speeding Tickets from Beyond the Grave

Drivers may frown on the officers who issue moving violations, but it's not easy being a traffic cop in San Francisco. As in many police departments around the nation, officers may be penalized for falling "below the curve" in issuing traffic citations, or even failing to meet a certain quota. We don't know what happens to these officers, but it must be something terrible. Some people claim that one poor officer is still writing traffic tickets in the afterlife. This cop pulls people over in Golden Gate Park and cites them for speeding, but when disgruntled drivers try to challenge the ticket in court, they learn that the officer died more than 10 years ago. Legend has it that if a cop trails you in the park, you should leave the park before pulling over. As you cross the border, the ghost officer will vanish.

Haunted Restrooms of the Bay Area

Just as San Francisco attracts strange people, it also seems to draw unusual ghosts—or at least some bizarre ghost stories. Whether or not they are true depends upon if you believe in spirits from the afterlife.

Some apparitions show up just when you want some privacy. Rumor has it that a 16- or 17-year-old boy haunts the third-floor men's room in Washington High School at 600 32nd Avenue. Students and teachers have reported seeing him standing by the stalls after school lets out. If you look away for a moment, he disappears. No one has any clue who he is, or why he's in the bathroom.

Another spirit frequents the ladies' room at the Village Oaks Shopping Center in Clayton, a town not far from San Francisco. When Richard Taylor, author of *Ghosts and Other Celebrities of Clayton*, leads the local Halloween Ghost Walk, he takes his tour groups through the restroom. He says the ghost is a

> *Rumor has it that a 16-year-old boy haunts the third-floor men's room in Washington High School.*

woman from the 1890s who got into a fight with her boyfriend in an outdoor dance pavilion that once stood on the site of the shopping center. According to Taylor, she later killed her boyfriend at a nearby creek.

The women who work in the nearby beauty parlor have encountered the ghost on their bathroom breaks. Psychics also say they sense her presence. A security guard noticed that someone had left the door to the women's room open. He went inside to investigate. As he glanced in the mirror, a face peered over his shoulder. He turned, but no one was there.

The Blue Lady

One of the most famous ghosts in San Francisco is the Moss Beach Distillery's "Blue Lady"—featured on NBC's *Unsolved Mysteries*. Built in the 1920s, the distillery kept San Francisco well stocked with bootlegged liquor during Prohibition. Alma, the bartender's wife, spent every evening at the distillery and always wore a blue flapper dress. On February 17, 1927, Alma disappeared. She was later found on the beach with a knife in her chest. Though the police never solved the case, many believe that her husband, the bartender, killed her when he discovered she was having an affair with the piano player.

Located on a cliff in Half Moon Bay, the Moss Beach Distillery now serves as a popular dining spot with a gorgeous view of the Pacific. The owner, John Barbour, didn't believe in the Blue Lady when he bought the property in 1990.

Now he says, "It's very clear the place is haunted and has been for some time. When you start looking at the experiences, they really pile up."

The Blue Lady behaves like a poltergeist, pulling ghostly pranks. She supposedly haunts both the men's and women's bathrooms, as well as the office, dining room, and storage areas. Some people claim to hear voices coming out of the dryer in the restroom. Staff members have reported checkbooks levitating and discovered wine barrels stacked in strange formations inside the locked storeroom. A member of Barbour's staff quit one day when all the computers booted up with the date February 17, 1927. Perhaps someone had sent a computer virus as a prank, but the manufacturers, who finally overhauled the system, couldn't account for what had happened.

Barbour finally got so tired of explaining the spooky goings-on that he printed a brochure about the Blue Lady called *The Distillery Times*. "You get to the point where you become blasé after a while. You just say, 'That's the Blue Lady,' " says Barbour.

Adolph Sutro

The visionary mining engineer Adolph Sutro came to San Francisco in 1850 aboard the steamship *California*. He built a small mill, the Sutro Metallurgical Works, in 1859 shortly after the discovery of the celebrated Comstock Lode— an enormous silver-mining region near Virginia City, Nevada. Sutro dreamed of engineering a four-mile-long mountain tunnel that would help drain water from the silver mines of the Comstock Lode. But Sutro's tunnel plan threatened William C. Ralston and William Sharon, who ran the Bank of California, which controlled the mine. The bankers frustrated Sutro's efforts to raise capital for the tunnel, until a fire swept through the mine, killing 45 men.

At an opera house near the mine, Sutro addressed the survivors and claimed that his tunnel would have allowed men to escape the fire. He asked the miners to buy stock in his tunnel plan, which he said, "would make you the power of this land, make powerless your oppressors, and break up your arch enemy, the California Bank."

The plan succeeded and Sutro started work on his tunnel in 1869. After completing the project in 1879, he sold his stake in the enterprise and invested in San Francisco real estate. The money from the tunnel funded Sutro's best-known engineering project, the luxurious Tropic Baths (see page 246). Sutro also purchased the old Rancho San Miguel near Twin Peaks. He bought up so much land that he once owned one-twelfth of the city. San Francisco had barren hills until the 1890s, when Sutro put unemployed citizens to work planting thousands of trees. Many of these trees still stand in the Sunset District's "Sutro Forest" on Mount Parnassus.

Sutro built his own house on a hilltop, now called Sutro Heights, overlooking the baths. The land affords a sweeping view of Ocean Beach, which stretches for miles toward the Santa Cruz Mountains. The property features classical statues, as well as Monterey pines, cypresses, and eucalyptus trees. Sutro was dedicated to creating spaces for everyone to enjoy, and so he opened his lawns and gardens to the public.

In 1894, Sutro ran for mayor of San Francisco. At that time, the Southern Pacific Railroad dominated California politics. Sutro had already opposed the railroad by building a competing electric train when Southern Pacific refused to reduce the fare on its steam line to five cents, so that working class people could visit the Sutro Baths.

Though wealthy, Sutro was a Jewish populist, which made him an outsider with respect to the reigning plutocracy. Nonetheless, he won the election on the populist "anti-octopus" ticket and served a two-year term as mayor. Sutro died in 1898, not long after he left office.

Sutro's elaborate Victorian Cliff House burned down in 1907, after surviving the 1906 earthquake. The current Cliff House, a rather plain structure, serves lunch and has recently been upgraded with a new viewing area. The hilltop where Sutro's house once stood is now a park called Sutro Heights. Though the house is gone, some of Sutro's trees and sculptures remain. After lunch at the new Cliff House, you can climb the hill to Sutro Heights for a spectacular view of Ocean Beach and the spooky water-soaked ruins of the Sutro Baths.

Sutro Baths

On a rocky shoreline at the northwestern edge of San Francisco lies the remains of Adolph Sutro's Tropic Baths. Sutro had a great fondness for bathing and back in the second half of the 19th century, when most people took one bath a week on Saturday night, Sutro insisted on bathing daily. This was considered slightly weird at the time. He even took a collapsible tub with him when he traveled and sent portable bathtubs to his children in college.

> *Sutro had a great fondness for bathing, and he insisted on bathing daily.*

To warm the chilly waters off the windy and foggy coast of San Francisco's Ocean Beach, Sutro built an enormous glass palace covering two acres of shoreline. With 600 tons of metal girders to hold the glass in place, the baths faced the ocean and included six swimming pools. Ingeniously engineered, the baths encompassed a saltwater aquarium and pools beneath the cliffs on the site. The water was channeled through a system of tunnels and canals, steam heated, and pumped into the pools. One of the big pools was filled with spray from waves at high tide.

Swimmers floated in the warm water, watching sunlight stream through the colored glass and the waves breaking just outside the windows. Sutro even built a tunnel into the nearby cliffs where visitors could watch the incoming waves hit the rocks below. The entire complex was protected by a stone wall that cut across the cove and reached north to a huge rock, where visitors could fish and explore the tide pools.

The swimming pools had diving platforms and water slides descending from the rafters. Swimmers could swing out over the water from trapeze-like rings attached to the ceiling. Observers watched swimming and diving contests from comfortable galleries while listening to Strauss waltzes. The pavilion also featured restaurants, a theater, a museum, rare plants, animals, and Egyptian artifacts. The upper terraces of the building held rooms filled with tropical plants, palm trees and exotic flowers, classical Greek and Roman statues and gigantic stuffed animals.

A number of writers have compared the Sutro Baths to the glamorous spas of Europe or the Roman baths. The entire pavilion could hold 25,000 people at a time. Sutro even installed an early Ferris Wheel, called the Firth Wheel, above the baths.

By 1937, the baths were losing money and so the main swimming pool was converted into an ice skating rink. Visitors still came to skate and look at Sutro's collection of antique music boxes, but by World War II the baths had fallen into disrepair. The building was closed and abandoned in the late 1950s. In 1966, a demolition crew was knocking down the glorious glass pavilion to build an apartment house complex, when a fire broke out, destroying what remained of the buildings.

The National Park Service now manages the remains of Adolph Sutro's Tropic Baths. You can explore this fantastic archaeological ruin and view the system of canals that carried water to the pools. Now filled with murky water, the pools are returning to salt marsh. Treading carefully along the edge where swimmers once dived, you can peer down at the reservoirs and tidal pools still filled by incoming waves. You can also venture into Sutro's tunnel through the seaside cliffs for a closer view of the surf.

In the Footsteps of Sam Spade

Dashiell Hammett, author of *The Maltese Falcon*, lived in San Francisco from 1921 to 1929—his most productive years as a writer. Drawing on his job as an investigator in the San Francisco office of Pinkerton's Detective Agency, Hammett penned the best hardboiled detective fiction of the 1920s and launched an entire literary universe of tough guy detectives.

Unlike gentleman sleuth Sherlock Holmes, Hammett's detectives were regular men. They were rough and callous, but had their own code of honor. Their investigations followed the crime, money, greed, corruption, and shady business deals that took place—and still take place—in San Francisco.

Hammett, whom friends called "Dash," set many of his mysteries in San Francisco's foggy streets and dark alleyways. Author and historian Don Herron leads walking tours of the city, revisiting the real places where the author set his scenes. Wearing a trench coat and a fedora hat, Herron starts his four-hour "Dashiell Hammett" tour at the San Francisco Main Public Library, near the Eddy Street apartment that Hammett once shared with his wife Josephine. While working for Pinkerton's, Hammett read detective stories at the library and began submitting pieces to *The Black Mask*, a pulp detective magazine.

The tour stops at City Hall, where Sam Spade is called into the district attorney's office for questioning in *The Maltese Falcon*. On McAllister Street, Herron visits the scene of a shootout in Hammett's short story, "The Whois Kid." He brings visitors to the Charing Cross Apartments on Post Street, where Hammett first dreamed up Sam Spade, then leads them on to the address of the gumshoe's office on Sutter Street. The tour also visits the Clift, the St. Francis and the St. Francis Drake hotels, which are disguised, but easily recognizable in Hammett's fiction. A plaque on Burritt Street, a little alley off of Bush, reads: "On approximately this spot, Miles Archer, partner of Sam Spade, was done in by Brigid O'Shaughnessy." The Dashiell Hammett Tour also draws fans of Humphrey Bogart, who played Sam Spade in the film version of *The Maltese Falcon*. "I won't play the sap for you," says Herron, clenching his teeth and narrating bits of Spade's dialogue to Brigid O'Shaughnessy.

The tour ends on Ellis Street at John's Grill, an old chophouse where Hammett actually ate and wrote some of his stories. With dark wood paneling and jazz playing in the background, it's just the kind of place a tough detective would come to for a quiet lunch. Historic photographs of San Francisco hang on the walls, and the upstairs room boasts a collection of Hammett memorabilia. You can even eat "Sam Spade's Chops"—the "chops, baked potato and sliced tomatoes" that the detective orders at the chophouse in *The Maltese Falcon*. According to the menu, Hammett lived nearby at an apartment at Geary and Hyde and prowled the neighborhood at night like his detective Sam Spade.

The Wild Parrots of San Francisco

Visitors to San Francisco's Telegraph Hill are often astonished to find a noisy flock of brilliant green parrots roaming wild through the treetops. Most of the 130 birds belong to the species *aratinga erythrogenys*, commonly known as the cherry-headed conure or the red-masked parakeet.

A smaller flock of white-winged parakeets (*brotegeris versicolorus*) roosts along Dolores Street and has graced the Potrero Hill and Noe Valley neighborhoods since the early 1970s, as the rapidly multiplying cherry-head parrots pushed them out of the north end of the city. Both flocks attract faithful followers who feed them, but the cherry-headed parrots are more popular among city residents. Some people keep detailed journals chronicling the lives of individual birds.

San Francisco's parrots originally came from the west side of the Andes in southern Ecuador and the extreme north of Peru. Until 1993, it was legal to import wild-caught South American parrots and people could buy them in pet stores. They were inexpensive, but obviously unhappy in captivity. Some owners released the birds when they bit or created a ruckus, while others simply escaped. The parrots started to gather in a flock during the winter, and the group are growing in number. Parrot observer Mark Bittner says there were only 26 parrots when he first began counting them in October 1993. Some of the original birds still had quarantine bands around their legs.

According to Bittner, the parrots' year-round territory extends from the grassy Ferry Plaza area across from the downtown Ferry Building, to the eastern edge of the Presidio and the Laurel Heights neighborhood. The birds also frequent Washington Square Park and Fort Mason. They roam the neighborhoods, eating juniper berries, pine nuts, walnuts, blackberries, apples, loquats, strawberry guavas, pears, cotoneaster berries, English hawthorn, magnolia, and their favorite—cherry blossoms. They snack at birdfeeders, but they don't rely on them.

The parrots tolerate the chilly San Francisco weather and have survived at least one freeze without ill effects. Around the first day of summer, mother parrots lay their eggs, often in their favorite nesting trees, the eucalyptus and the non-native Canary Island date palm. Instead of building nests, the birds use holes in trees. These holes must be a certain size and height above the ground and must face a certain direction. Parrots have a maximum of four babies, who leave their nesting holes in early September. A similar flock of parrot lives in Chicago all year round.

The parrots don't seem to bother the native northern California birds, but hawks and occasionally housecats prey on them. Every evening just before dusk, the parrots gather in the trees in Ferry Park, where they scream and carry on loudly. If you are lucky enough to get close to them, they are fond of safflower seeds.

Kim Corbin Launches National Skipping Craze

It all started with a simple exercise routine. In April 1999, Kim Corbin of San Francisco began skipping to get in shape. She lost 25 pounds. Anywhere else in the country, her passion for skipping may have gone no further than that. But being a San Franciscan, Corbin decided to start a movement. "To share the joy of skipping with the world," she launched the website iskip.com. "Before I knew it," she writes, "my unusual vision of starting a national adult skipping movement had become a reality."

Corbin now organizes group skips and hosts an online skipping community. Her movement claims hundreds, if not thousands, of adherents worldwide, including a strange character known as Peter Pan—a pixyish 50-something man in a green Lycra costume, who visited San Francisco to receive the 2001 Webby Award for weirdest website.

San Francisco's Mysterious Walls

In the hills to the east of the San Francisco Bay are a number of ancient stone walls that have puzzled archaeologists for over a century. The walls are in haphazard sections, from 10 meters to over half a mile long, with stones up to a meter high and a meter wide. The reason for the wall's construction remains a mystery—the wall is too short for ramifications and too random to serve as containment fences. Over the years, there have been a number of theories about the stones: they are solstice sites built by Druids; Native Americans were ordered to construct them to instill a Christian work ethic in them; the walls were built by traveling Asians or by Chinese workers after the gold rush. Although these versions of events have become part of local legend, a conclusive explanation remains elusive.

SOURCES

Adams, Charles F. *The Magnificent Rogues of San Francisco.* Palo Alto: Pacific Books, 1998.

Asbury, Herbert. *The Barbary Coast.* New York: Knopf, 1933.

Auerbach, D. M., W.W. Darrow, H.W. Jaffe, and J.W. Curran. *The American Journal of Medicine,* No. 76, 1984.

Ayer. *Gold and Sunshine.* New York: Gorham, 1922.

Bailey, Janet. *The Great San Francisco Trivia and Fact Book.* Cumberland House Publishing, 1999.

Bain, Donald. *The Control of Candy Jones.* Playboy Press, 1976.

Benson, Heidi. "Arcata police log gets writer's poetic caress," *San Francisco Chronicle,* August 15, 2004.

Bittner, Mark. *The Wild Parrots of Telegraph Hill.* Three Rivers Press, 2005.

Borthwick, J. D. *The Gold Hunters.* 1924.

Boulware, Jack. *San Francisco Bizarro.* New York: St. Martin's, 2000.

Bower, Bruce. "Ishi's Long Road Home" *Science News,* January 8, 2000.

Boyd, Nan Alamilla. *Wide-Open Town: A History of Queer San Francisco to 1965.* Berkeley and Los Angeles: University of California Press, 2004.

Brechin, Gray. *Imperial San Francisco: Urban Power, Earthly Ruin.* Berkeley: University of California Press, 1999.

Burrows, Edwin G. and Mike Wallace. *Gotham: A History of New York to 1898.* Oxford: Oxford University, 1999.

Caen, Herb. "Comme See Comme Saw," *San Francisco Chronicle,* May 1, 1995.

Cavalieri, Nate. "Love on the Run," *SF Weekly.*

Driver, Nick. "Old Chinatown's Deep, Dark Secrets," *San Francisco Examiner,* April 18, 2002.

Faas, Ekbert. *Young Robert Duncan: Portrait of the Artist as a Homosexual in Society.* Santa Barbara: Black Sparrow Press, 1983.

Ford, Dave. "FrontRunners," *San Francisco Chronicle,* September 2, 2004.

Ford, Dave. "Strange but True," *San Francisco Chronicle,* January 23, 2004.

Friend, Tad. "Jumpers: The fatal grandeur of the Golden Gate Bridge," *New Yorker,* October 13, 2003.

Garchik, Leah. "El Cerrito Artist's BraBall Inspires a Show of Support," *San Francisco Chronicle,* March 16, 2001.

Garchik, Leah. "The Future in Fine Dining," *San Francisco Chronicle,* January 10, 2001.

Garchik, Leah. "Wrap It Up And Send It To Jesse," *San Francisco Chronicle,* February 5, 1996.

Garcia, Ken. *San Francisco Chronicle,* June 28, 2001.

Goffman, Ken. *Counterculture Through the Ages.* New York: Villard, 2004.

Haines, J.D. "The King of Quacks," *Skeptical Inquirer,* May 2002.

Hall, Carl T. "Gorilla's life in human hands: UCSF doctors remove lung of sick zoo ape in one-of-a-kind surgery—now wait begins," *San Francisco Chronicle,* May 8, 2004.

Hall, Carl T. "Medical heroics not just for humans" *San Francisco Chronicle*, May 17, 2004.

Holdredge, Helen. *Mammy Pleasant*. San Carlos: Nourse, 1961.

Hoskyns, Barney. *Beneath the Diamond Sky: Haight-Ashbury 1965–1970*. New York: Simon & Schuster, 1997.

Issel, William and Robert W. Cherny. *San Francisco 1865-1932: Politics, Power, and Urban Development*. Berkeley: University of California Press, 1986.

Johnson, Susan Lee. *Roaring Camp: The Social World of the California Gold Rush*. New York: W. W. Norton, 2000.

Jonnes, Jill. *Hep-Cats, Narcs, and Pipe Dreams*. New York: Scribner, 1996.

Kingman, Russ. *A Pictorial Life of Jack London*. New York: Crown, 1979.

Kinney, Christian. "San Francisco Art Institute," in *Discovery Channel Adventures Haunted Holidays*. Discovery Communications, 1999.

Knight, Heather. "Backyard Haunts: From Nob Hill to Napa, it's spooky how many tales of ghost are floating around," *San Francisco Chronicle*, October 26, 2001.

Kurth, Peter. *Isadora: A Sensational Life*. Back Bay Books, 2002.

Lee, Martin A. and Bruce Shlain. *Acid Dreams*. New York: Grove Press, 1985.

Levy, Dan. "Downed Doggie Sign Fixable" San Francisco Chronicle, March 4, 2001.

Lynch, April. "The Mystery Tipster, Strange de Jim, Tips His Hand at Last," *San Francisco Chronicle*, 1997.

Martin, Glen. *San Francisco Chronicle*, April 27, 2004.

May, Antoinette. *Haunted Houses of California:* World Wide Publishing, 1993.

Mencken, H. L. *Heathen Days: 1890–1936*. Baltimore: Johns Hopkins University Press, 1996.

Menzies, Gavin. *1421: The Year China Discovered America*. William Morrow & Co., 2003.

Monaghan, Jay. *Chile, Peru, and the California Gold Rush of 1849*. Berkeley: University of California Press, 1973.

Montandon, Pat. *The Intruders*. Coward, McCann & Geoghegan, Inc., 1975.

Moss, Andrew R. "'AIDS Without End,'" *The New York Review of Books,* August 18, 1988.

O'Reilly, James, Larry Habegger, and Sean O'Reilly. *Travelers' Tales: San Francisco*. Travelers' Tales Guides, 2002.

Pogash, Carol. "Myth of the 'Twinkie Defense,'" *San Francisco Chronicle*, November 23, 2003.

Rosenfeld, Seth. "Mario Savio's FBI Odyssey," *San Francisco Chronicle Magazine*. October 10, 2004.

Said, Carolyn. *San Francisco Chronicle*, August 6, 2004.

Schevitz, Tanya. "Flesh-eating plants so beguiling they lure 3 men to commit crime," *The San Francisco Examiner*, April 16, 1995.

Schwartz, Stephen. *From West to East: California and the Making of the American Mind*. New York: Free Press, 1998.

Starn, Orin. *Ishi's Brain: In Search Of America's Last "Wild" Indian*. New York: Norton, 2004.

Starr, Kevin. *Americans and the California Dream: 1850-1915*. New York: Oxford, 1973.

Stevenson, Robert Louis. *The Wrecker*. 1892.

Weeks, Dr. David and Jamie James. *Eccentrics: A Study of Sanity and Strangeness*. New York: Vallard, 1995.

Yollin, Patricia. "Looking back at history: Zoo turns 75—Three quarters of a century of wild tales," *San Francisco Chronicle*, July 29, 2004.

Yollin, Patricia. "Rowdy gals face a tamer S.F. lifestyle: After escaping death, sister grizzlies are en route to zoo," *San Francisco Chronicle*, October 3, 2004.

Yollin, Patricia. "Zoo penguins intent on futile 'migration' S.F. flock swims round and round in pool," *San Francisco Chronicle*, January 16, 2003.

WEB SITES

archive.aclu.org
goodvibes.com/
iskip.com/about_iskip/about_
   skipper.html
lifesizemousetrap.com
members.aol.com/strange777/herb.html
members.aol.com/strangecastro
news.bbc.co.uk/
seattlepi.nwsource.com/national/
   skip01.html
www.alcatrazhistory.com/alcesc1.htm
www.artcarfest.com
www.billboardliberation.com
www.blackpanther.org/legacynew.htm
www.burningman.com
www.bwfly.com/watchbison
www.cacophony.org
www.carpenoctem.tv/haunt/ca
www.cdnn.info/safety/s040816a/
   s040816a.html
www.citylights.com/CLIf.html

www.cockettes.com/history1.html
www.colma.ca.gov/briefhis.html
www.crimelibrary.com/
www.culannshounds.com/madpiper.htm
www.cyclecide.com
www.dealguitars.com/deal.htm
www.disinfo.com/archive/pages/
   dossier?id366/pg1
www.doggiediner.com
www.dolphinclub.org
www.dribbleglass.com/subpages/laws
www.fabiangonzalez.com/photos/chu.htm
www.faultline.org/place/2002/01/
   hammett.html
www.fractalcow.com/bert/bert.htm
www.frameline.org/festival/22nd/
   awards.html
www.fvza.org/history1.html
www.geocities.com/capitolhill/
   congress/2503/main.html
www.geocities.com/mepleasant.geo/mep.
   html
www.glbtq.com/social-
   sciences/san_francisco2.html
www.humournet.com/collage.
   archives/collage255.txt
www.lbl.gov/ehs/esg/96ser/
   96serch9ser.html
www. mercurynews.com
www.mistersf.com
www.museumca.org/goldrush/
   getin-pr01.html

www.newsoftheweird.com
www.newsreview.com/issues/chico/2002-
   03-14/cover.asp
www.nps.gov/alcatraz/indian2.html
www.pbs.org/weta/thewest/people/a_c/
   crocker.htm
www.popsubculture.com/pop/bio_
   project/allen_ginsberg.html
www.randomhouse.com/features/
   steel/profile.html
www.rooknet.com/beatpage/
   writers/kaufman.html
www.saintstupid.com/parade.htm
www.Salon.com
www.sfgate.com
www.sfghosthunt.com/employeebios.html
www.sfheart.com/cohen_bio.html
www.sfhistoryencyclopedia.com/
   articles/o/olderFremont.html
www.sfmuseum.org
www.sfweekly.com
www.snopes.com
www.sonnet.com/eqdir/clamper/
   skunks.html
www.srl.org
www.tattooarchive.com/
www.thesisters.org
www.time.com
www.west.net/~wwmr/gemston1
www.wired.com/news/conflict/
   0,2100,47450,00.html
www.zpub.com

Acknowledgments

We would like to acknowledge our editors, Cheryl Thomas and Frank Hopkinson, and the many folks who took the time to suggest story ideas—Antonio Bettencourt, Valentina Bettencourt, Sadie Kaufman, Jonathan Lethem, Carol Queen, Roxxie Rosen, whose technical support saved the day, Robert Lawrence, who brainstormed a deluge of oddities by the Bay, and John Gilmore, who not only provided stories, but food, luxury accommodations, a printer, and the pleasure of his company during the project's most crucial gestation phase.

This book is dedicated to Ann's literary auntie, Lauretta Bassert, who encouraged her to be a writer. We also salute all the self-identified and self-made freaks. San Francisco would never have been possible without you.